Ear Training for Twentieth-Century Music

MICHAEL L.
FRIEDMANN

Ear Training
for
Twentieth-
Century
Music

Yale University Press   New Haven and London

Designed by James J. Johnson and
set in Futura & Times Roman types by
Keystone Typesetting, Inc., Orwigsburg,
Pennsylvania.
Printed in the United States of America by
BookCrafters, Inc., Chelsea, Michigan.

Library of Congress Cataloging-in-Publication Data

Friedmann, Michael L., 1946–
    Ear training for twentieth-century music /
Michael L. Friedmann.
        p.   cm.
    Includes bibliographical references.
    ISBN 0–300–04536–0. —
    ISBN 0–300–04537–9 (pbk.)

    1. Ear Training. 2. Music—Theory—
20th century. I. Title.
MT35.F87 1990
781.4′24—dc20   89–39641
                                                      CIP/MN

10 9 8 7 6 5 4 3 2

Contents

Abbreviations

CAS	contour adjacency series
CC	contour class
CIS	contour interval series
ex(x).	example(s)
ic	interval class
i(n)	unordered pitch class interval n
ill(s).	illustration(s)
I_n	pitch class inversion with sum n
$I_{+/-}{}^p{}_n$	pitch inversion with sum $+/-$ n
ip<$+/-$n>	ordered pitch interval $+/-$ n
ip(n)	unordered pitch interval n
M.I.	modal interval
M.O.	modal order
pc	pitch class
rip series	registral pitch interval series
sc	set class
T_n	transposition at the pitch class "distance" n
T^p_n	pitch transposition at the distance of pitch interval n

Exercises

Preface

This book will be used primarily in the classroom, but I hope the musician who seeks an improved perception of twentieth-century music will be able to work on its exercises and concepts independently or with a colleague. At least two types of courses could profitably use the book as a text: a course in the analysis of twentieth-century music that has an ear training component, or "lab"; and an advanced course in an ear training sequence. The first of these, taught over a full year, presents the best opportunity for coordinating theoretical, analytical, and aural activities.

In my own teaching I have found that even a full semester of work on the activities proposed in this book does not suffice to complete them all. I have never found time to explore fully chapters 5 and 6, and often I have found that the work of chapter 3 also gets short shrift. The student who becomes thoroughly engaged with the exercises of chapter 1 and the musical examples of appendix 1 will have a worthwhile encounter with twentieth-century melodies and harmonies. But to get the most out of this book the student will not only master the exercises in all its chapters, but seek a flexible and expansive application of its concepts. In other words, the depth and extent of analytic structuring that should accompany the "calisthenic" exploration of the exercises is entirely up to the teacher. If the material of chapter 2 has not been mastered, there is little point in expecting positive results from a study of chapter 4. Chapters 3 and 6 offer some exceptions to this "building block" approach because the materials of contour and mode constitute special topics.

Because of the difficulty of the material, steady, sustained, and logical work is of the essence. Most of the exercises require at least two people. In a classroom dictation the teacher will often be the player, but two students working together can profitably exchange the roles of player and listener. Despite the overall structuring role of the teacher, who often acts as the "instrument" advancing the student's ends, the text is directed toward the student. Exercises that can be done by one student alone are so labeled.

It is my earnest hope that teachers and other readers will not merely plod through the book's exercises mechanically, but will use them as a stimulus for other work, emphasizing those facets of the book that draw the students into the closest possible contact with the music. Although an improvement in the mechanics of ear training and musicianship is an inevitable and desirable outcome of doing these exercises, one even closer to my heart is that the reader will be more intensely engaged with the music of the twentieth century. After internalizing the theme of Schoenberg's Piano Concerto through the exercises in chapters 1, 3, and 6, I hope the reader will feel motivated to listen to and study the rest of the piece, so that Schoenberg's ambition, that musicians and audiences would whistle his melodies as they did those of Tchaikovsky, might be realized.

Acknowledgments

The eight classes of students with whom I have tried out these materials are the main assistants I have had in writing this book. Both in their specific suggestions on how to make my ideas clearer and in simply providing the data on what works and what does not, they have shown great enthusiasm and patience, and generated much of the inspiration to complete my work.

Among the individual students who have been most helpful are Richard Kurth, who lived in my house and helped me edit the manuscript, thus functioning more as a colleague than as a student; Bruce Nichols, whose experience in both music and publishing gave his enthusiasm and support extra credibility; John Rose, whose grasp of substance and insights into style helped me greatly, as did his proofreading of musical examples; Hugh Livingston, for his work on the musical examples; and Shannon Scott, Alison Wells, Ursula Smith, Michael Amory, and Katie Lansdale, for their feedback, both positive and negative.

Among my colleagues, Christopher Hasty commiserated when there were setbacks, and steadfastly presented the analytic ear as the goal of ear training. Allen Forte gave immediate encouragement when I first envisioned the project. Thanks are due to the Griswold Faculty Research Fund and the Frederick W.

Hilles Publication Fund of Yale University for defraying the cost of securing permission to reproduce examples from the music of Schoenberg, Stravinsky, Bartók, and Debussy, as well as of transcribing, proofreading, and photocopying the examples. My editor at Yale University Press, Fred Kameny, was enthusiastic, helpful, and idealistic.

My wife, Deborah Davis, prodded me effectively on the many occasions when my own energies waned, and set an impressive example of scholarly persistence in her own research on Chinese society.

Introduction

The community of musicians has never before been confronted with the level of fragmentation that exists today. Analytic method is divorced from musical reflex, composers from performers, and conventional repertoire from new repertoire. In this century these polarities have developed because of the momentum of compartmentalization—a trend that has played an important role in many aspects of culture, education, and technology. Countertrends in specific areas of human endeavor and in the work of extraordinary, multifaceted people have asserted themselves sporadically, but not with the same, sustained persistence as the overriding tendency toward specialization.

A lack of mutual understanding is apparent both among and within the major groups of participants in musical life: composers, performers, theorists, and audiences. Most contemporary composers write mainly for their colleagues and a narrowly defined group of listeners in major cities and universities. Their music is usually played by a group of specialists able only rarely to convey the expressive content of the new music. These specialists are trained to meet the extraordinary technical demands of the music, but their work shows a linguistic incompetence—an inability to grasp the gesture and intent of the music. A similarly uncomprehending performance of older music would be dismissed by the most casual listener. From the performer's perspective, the technical difficulties are so problematic that an expressive relationship to the music is often hard to attain. Such performance problems in turn make the audience's appreciation of the music improbable.

The barriers separating composers, performers, and audiences have existed as long as there have been concerts, but they have become more formidable since the breakthroughs of the first half of the twentieth century exemplified in the music of Schoenberg, Berg, Webern, Debussy, Bartók, and Stravinsky. In their departure from a tonally centered language of functional harmony, composers of this century have led music in a great variety of directions, and no source of common linguistic cues has replaced those of eighteenth- and nineteenth-century tonality. Because of this diversity listeners and performers have had great difficulty in coming to grips with the music and integrating it into the basic concert repertoire. The lack of a clearly perceivable common style, language, and aesthetic is one important source of both the richness and the difficulty of the music of this century.

Although the music of diatonic tonality presented structural signals relating to overall syntax as well as to expressive effect in each sonority, or at least in each phrase, the music of the twentieth century opens up multiple associations, only some of which prove to be of central relevance to the continuity of the music. A comparison of even the most obvious features of two examples can highlight the problem that performers and listeners may encounter with radical twentieth-century music. The opening of the overture to Mozart's *Marriage of*

Int.1. Mozart: *Marriage of Figaro*, Overture

Figaro (ill. int.1), like innumerable other examples, establishes a tonal center and a network of relationships among the seven possible diatonic pitches and the five additional chromatic pitches. The music presents itself within a rhythmic periodicity, a balanced, multileveled framework of antecedent and consequent within which future events can be understood.

Int.2. Schoenberg: *Pierrot lunaire,* opening

The opening of Schoenberg's *Pierrot lunaire* (ill. int.2), on the other hand, offers a wide range of *types* of possibilities for interpretive focus; the listener must in fact be aware of these multiple musical parameters to gain access to the musical content.

Int.2a. "½ step" displaced

These musical factors include the following: (1) The melodic shape and quarter-note pulse imply a motion toward D, the fourth pitch. (2) The trajectory from the first note of the seven-note piano figure to the last shows a half-step motion, "displaced" by an octave, from G-sharp to G (ill. int.2a).

Int.2b. Whole-tone scale at outset

(3) The first five piano pitches plus the first violin pitch make up a whole-tone scale (ill. int.2b).

(4) The nine pitch classes of the first measure can be divided into groups of six and three, drawn from the two whole-tone scales (ill. int.2c).

Int.2c. 6:3 whole-tone breakdown

Aug.   Dim.

Int.2d. Augmented-diminished

(5) The seven-note figure in the piano begins with an augmented triad and ends with a diminished triad (ill. int.2d).

(6) The only pitch classes *not* present in this bar are B, A, and F.

Int.2e. Contour: "Down-then-up"

(7) The contour "down-then-up" occurs twice among adjacent three-note groups in the seven-note figure and is also heard as the overall shape of the melody (ill. int.2e).

One could certainly make similar observations about the example from Mozart. But its elements would be subsumed under the power of the tonal relationships. The lack of a unifying force in the Schoenberg comparable to these tonal relationships makes other musical parameters gain strength and importance through their independence. All seven of the observations made above are of the kind that can be demonstrated to have centrality in other works by Schoenberg. Whether any of them have central relevance in this piece is a purely contextual issue, to be investigated as the music continues. Because there is no dependable set of cues to single out the main strand of continuity in the music, the listener must find a personally convincing path by repeated listening rather than by generating an instant framework of expectations, as would have been possible in the Mozart.

There are two strategies for gaining access to twentieth-century music: one can use enhanced instinctual responses to music to replace a habitual adherence to expectations based exclusively on older music; and one can refine the mind-ear apparatus, to give intellectual support to the instinctual, aural ability. By implication, one will also establish a descriptive vocabulary and descriptive categories that are either value-free or uniquely appropriate to the newer music.

To make the listener conversant with the complexities of new music and to bridge the gaps separating composers, performers, and audiences, I have chosen a modest but critical area: ear training. By making this choice I have taken a narrowly technical approach to a problem that must also be addressed on broader, aesthetic grounds, but for the practitioners of music this is a necessary starting point. Although ear training has long been accepted in the curricula of schools of music, problems of twentieth-century musicianship appear somewhere near the end of ear training courses because they are viewed as among the most difficult the student may encounter, and the particular character of their difficulties is almost never addressed. Through unusual gifts such as absolute pitch or photographic memory, a few students find themselves able to take a melody by Schoenberg in dictation or memorize it. The rest are relatively helpless when confronted with this sort of task.

Ear training exercises dealing with tonal music—singing, dictation, improvisation—are at least implicitly connected with the structures of tonality through the labeling devices and mechanisms for linguistic understanding generated by the theories of tonal music. In ill. int.1, for example, the immediate perception of a tonic pitch allows the listener to define the scale degrees of the high and low points of the melody, and to hear the arpeggiation of the tonic triad in the first three bars and the harmonic progression of dominant to tonic underlying mm. 6–7. Because theories of twentieth-century music have been presented so abstractly to performers, a comparable structuring process for this music has seemed unlikely to be achieved. Therefore, whatever efforts have been applied to ear training for twentieth-century music have been in the area of musical calisthenics—exercises for facility and memorization that lack the benefit of any linguistic structure.

In this book I attempt to use the calisthenic reflexes of the student as a starting point, but then to reinforce these reflexes with a structured approach that functions analogously to the scales, chord progressions, and counterpoint of tonal music. Instead of viewing the theories of twentieth-century music as more complex than the theories of tonality, I view them as more basic; in a sense they precede tonality, which is a special interpretation of the twelve pitch classes. The materials and skills developed in this book address the more general and fundamental material, before the special filter of tonality is applied to them as an overriding structural point of departure.

But adopting a more basic approach to materials does not make them any easier to digest. Twentieth-century music is arguably more difficult to interpret and grasp than the art music of earlier centuries: the materials and processes are far more diverse, the compositional approach is far more contextually based, with few concessions to a priori principles, and the physical density of musical information is far greater. It is essential that we begin working to achieve the same level of aural mastery of twentieth-century music as has been attained for earlier music. The progress made in the ear training of musicians in hearing and grasping the structural principles of twentieth-century music can be considered a measuring stick, both of the accessibility of the music and of the relevance of theories that serve as partial explanations for its coherence.

In developing the concepts that underlie this book I have reexamined what is meant when it is said that someone has a good ear. One prototype is the conductor who can discern in the densest orchestral texture a fault of intonation or rhythm. Another is the composer who can imagine instrumental balances and pitch combinations as if the performers were present. Still another is the listener who can give an account of the serial structure of a twelve-tone piece on one hearing without having seen the score. A less tangible but equally meaningful concept of "ear" is exemplified by the listener who can describe a relationship or process that provides the structural underpinning of a piece without being able to account for specific, detailed relationships.

We almost always know what it means for someone to have a good ear, but we have difficulty redefining this meaning for ourselves, and even greater difficulty explaining it to others. The only reasonable conclusion one can draw is that every good musician finds his or her own kind of good ear. I like to think that this book gives support to many kinds of good ear, but it would be naive to assume that every good musician could master all the exercises in this book, or that anyone who did would have achieved the proficiency associated with every kind of good ear.

I have chosen to define a good ear as one that perceives and retains musical structures and understands their role in a musical *transformation* or other compositional process. The musical structure can be a single pitch but is more likely to be a group of two or more pitches. To perceive such a musical structure one must first *segment* it from its surroundings in the musical continuity, so that it becomes a unit with sufficient internal integrity to be independently scrutinized, and then *identify* characteristics that can later be used to liken or contrast the unit to others. These characteristics may relate to the unit's harmonic content, or to such aspects as contour, temporal or registral order of intervals, or durational pattern.

A good ear is an ideal toward which all musicians work in some fashion. Its attainment can be manifested in many ways: when a violinist plays in tune, when a pianist performs a complex piece accurately from memory, when a composer writes a piece that "feels" as if it has the right proportions. Clearly, a good ear as defined here is one that goes beyond the mechanics of accurate dictation or precisely pitched singing: it enables the listener to perform acts of at least rudimentary analysis without consulting the score. Although the most accomplished practitioners of tonal analysis can articulate penetrating insights into musical structure without the aid of a score, analysts of twentieth-century music have never held strongly that their more arcane analyses can be accomplished "by ear." One of the long-range goals of this book is to challenge the assumption that analysis by ear is impossible, owing to the abstract nature of twentieth-century music and the analytic methods applied to it. I have chosen the topics of this book to help the student acquire an ear that can deal analytically with the materials of twentieth-century music.

Although this book is meant to be a pedagogical text, its subject matter demands that it be also a theoretical one; much of the book is therefore devoted to defining and elaborating theoretical concepts as well as exercising them by means of abstract examples and musical illustrations from the literature. Scholars and critics have failed to agree on a focus for listening to the music of this century. However eclectic one attempts to be, the results are inevitably the outcome of personal aesthetic choices. This book is no exception: it represents my conviction that the precise articulation of structural relations provides the basic foundation for twentieth-century music, and that perceiving them is a precondition for understanding affective content and gesture.

Chapter 1 of this book offers a blueprint for exercises that give practice to purely "calisthenic" capacities and their application to the musical examples; chapters 2–6 present a theoretical framework and exercises in its comprehension for the student. In the first chapter students sing, play, memorize, and take in dictation melodies by Schoenberg, Debussy, Bartók, and Stravinsky, much as they would melodies by earlier composers. This is done partly to cultivate a matter-of-fact attitude about mastering these materials, and partly to help the student find a foothold in this literature. The examples are chosen for their musical value, and I hope that practicing the calisthenic exercises will encourage the student to gain familiarity with the entire compositions. It cannot be overemphasized that the student should always return to the first chapter after completing the exercises in the following ones. Continuing exercise of the calisthenic faculties will demonstrate that these faculties draw on a reservoir that is replenished by more abstract and analytical work. Memorization should be stressed not merely for its own sake, but as a way of sustaining musical and intellectual concentration over time. In addition, memorizing is a first step in dealing with a musical phrase—an effective and valid means for the intelligent training of aural skills.

In chapter 2, I introduce ways of perceiving the relations of two pitches: as concrete musical phenomena in *pitch space* and, in the more abstract *pitch class space,* as *types* of phenomena. I also elaborate on the concept of a two-note harmonic type (dyad) as a generalization of different two-note melodic successions, and suggest relevant drills.

Chapter 3 deals with temporal and spatial order, and introduces processes (such as *transposition* and *inversion*) by which the constituents of a two-note unit are related to the constituents of another. The chapter also treats the subject of *melodic contour,* the sense in which melodic elements relate to each other in time and space independently of specific pitch and interval factors: relative order in time and space is studied, rather than absolute measurements of frequency and interval. Two descriptive tools are developed that act as levels of generality in precisely relating melodic elements with equivalent or inverted contours.

Chapter 4 uses material from the two preceding ones to deal with trichords. It introduces the concepts of set class and interval content, as well as various characterizations of the twelve transpositionally and inversionally equivalent three-note set types familiar from "atonal" theory. Because improvising with these materials will help the student crystallize them in mind and ear, the exercises in chapter 4 make the processes of transposition and inversion the subjects of improvisation, not merely of identification.

In chapter 5, I extend the concepts and exercises of chapter 4 into the area of tetrachords, of which the greater number (there are twenty-nine transpositionally and inversionally equivalent types) and consequently subtler differences require more elaborate kinds of characterization. I suggest different methods of grouping the twenty-nine transpositionally and inversionally equivalent tetrachords into "families," as a bridge for the student toward recognizing specific tetrachords.

Chapter 6 goes one step further, by dealing with selected larger sets of as many as eight elements. This chapter, as well as some of the material in the appendixes, is designed for the most ambitious and accomplished students. Among the topics discussed are pentachords, hexachords, and septachords that recur with particular frequency in the literature, and categories within which such larger sets can be accommodated.

Lest the reader assume that this book is concerned exclusively with rigorously "atonal" and twelve-tone music, chapter 6 also addresses different kinds of modes, especially as they are used by Debussy, Bartók, and Stravinsky. Simply put, modes are larger sets treated somewhat stably, and they demonstrate a "flattening" of pitch and pitch class space. Modal treatment of pitch material as presented here functions analogously to the concept of contour presented in chapter 3. The concept of modal order reintroduces the possibility of a tonal center, and the idea of modal interval is presented as an alternative to pitch interval and pitch class interval.

Appendix 1 includes numerous musical examples: three sections of increasingly difficult melodies, one section of two-part selections, and one section of three- and four-part selections. It drills various skills from earlier chapters in the context of some of these examples.

The activities of this book immerse the student in the radical music of the first half of the twentieth century. The student who has completed them will be able to describe musical events and processes in a somewhat analytical manner. More important, the intuitive sources of musicianship, often thrown into disarray because of the discontinuities between the art music of this century and the music of the past, will presumably have been replenished and brought into a more flexible relationship with the student's analytic faculties.

The work of five theorists of "atonal" music plays a central role in the intellectual foundations of this book. I hope the book will serve in turn to introduce their ideas to musicians who might otherwise find their work remote and formidable. Allen Forte's *Structure of Atonal Music* established a labeling system for the elements, structures, and processes of post-tonal music. More recently, in his writings dealing with the music of "transition" (works of Liszt, Wagner, Mahler, Scriabin), Forte has extended Schenkerian concepts of prolongation into the area of set class arpeggiation, tying motive and harmony together in ways that transcend triadic tonality. John Rahn's *Basic Atonal Theory* has further clarified the labeling structure, and emphasized a hierarchy of structures, from general to particular, for describing pitch relationships. David Lewin's work has focused on process rather than musical object, and has been of great importance in showing the dynamism of post-tonal musical relationships. Of all theorists of twentieth-century music, Lewin is the most nearly global in his paradigms for overall structure. Robert Morris's recent book *Composition with Pitch Classes,* though primarily a guide to post-tonal composition, embraces the areas of pitch class, pitch, contour, and mode in ways that are relevant to the full range of twentieth-century music. Christopher

Hasty's articles are perhaps closest to the enterprise of this book, in that he is preoccupied with the detailed hearing that brings coherence to the musical phrase, and to the process of segmentation that is central to defining musical elements.

In view of this theoretical underpinning, some readers will find my selection of intellectual structures too challenging; others will find the intellectual scope overly modest. Depending on their aims and backgrounds, students will use this book either as an introduction to the theories of twentieth-century music or as an ear training book that incorporates familiar theoretical structures. In any event, although an informed ear is not the only basis for perceiving and interpreting music, it is clearly an essential tool for the confidently aware musician.

Ear Training for Twentieth-Century Music

1 *Calisthenics*

The danger of applying a highly structured approach to ear training is that the naming process necessary for intellectualizing will block immediacy of apprehension, and that the structuring process will be a handicap rather than an aid. While absorbing the intellectual concepts and practicing the abstract exercises scattered throughout later chapters, the student must therefore work simultaneously on the more "calisthenic" exercises presented in this chapter.

Because all musicians bring considerable musical intuition to a study like this one, it seems appropriate to use that equipment rather than disregard it. This chapter consequently presumes the ability to repeat melodies vocally and write them down, to sing chords from bottom to top, to hear relations between adjacent pitches over time—faculties that have long been exercised by musicians in relation to earlier repertoire.

The first stages of work with the examples contained in appendix 1 are performance, repetition, and memorization of the single-line melodic excerpts. The suggested steps are as follows:

EXERCISE 1.1: Singing by imitation

The phrase elements of a melody are played by a pianist or other instrumentalist; sing them on "la" without a score; then accumulate consecutive phrase elements. Accuracy in intonation and rhythm should be the goal.

A concept crucial to improving melodic perception is the twofold notion of adjacency, or proximity: pitches may be adjacent in the temporal progression of the melody; or pitches may be adjacent in pitch space (separated by one or two half-steps), though not necessarily adjacent in time. Both concepts of proximity are useful in rehearsing the singing and hearing of melodies. By accurately singing the intervals that separate successive pitches one gains a sure sense of melodic continuity, and by hearing over temporally longer spans to sing spatially adjacent pitches one gains a greater sense of the integrity of the melody, especially in dealing with disjunct melodic lines. This is as true for melodic hearing in music of the tonal period as in twentieth-century music, and finds special application in "compound melodies." In Mozart's Sonata in C

1.1. Mozart: Sonata, K. 545, beginning

Major, K. 545 (ill. 1.1), we are of course interested in the intervals between successive tones of the melody (C and E, E and G, G and B). But the stepwise voice-leading relations of the opening C, the next downbeat, B, and the C two beats later contribute most significantly not only to establishing the meter but to the cohesion of these two bars of the melody.

Similarly, in the example from Schoenberg (ill. 1.2), although the large intervals formed by the successive tones of the melody constitute one of the

1.2. Schoenberg: String Quartet no. 3, slow movement, first violin

melody's principal attributes, it is the whole-step motion (high C to A-sharp, A-sharp to G-sharp, and low A to B) that is both easier to perceive and more critical to our grasp of melodic continuity.

EXERCISE 1.2: Hearing spatially adjacent pitches

After hearing a melody several times, attempt to sing all pairs of pitches separated by a whole-step or less and to sing them *before and after* successfully singing the whole melody, as in exercise 1.1. The following examples are among those that can be used: nos. 23, 46, 66, 72, 74, 102, 110, 111 and 112, 113, 120, and 130 (violin and cello to be done separately).

EXERCISE 1.3: Memorization (for one)

Perform the melody from memory on the piano or possibly another instrument, and then sing it, one phrase element at a time. (It cannot be overstressed that memorizing a phrase element gives a clear picture of the overall shape of the melody and its large-scale relationships that cannot be replicated in the analytically oriented exercises of later chapters.)

In the hearing of chords, the only ordering available is spatial (bottom to top or top to bottom). The following exercise is therefore of great importance:

EXERCISE 1.4: Hearing verticalities (with variant for one)

After hearing a simultaneity of two to four pitches over a span of as many as seventeen half-steps played on the piano, sing the pitches in spatial order: bottom to top, then top to bottom. The pianist can contrive these sonorities—they need not be taken from the examples. At an early stage of working on this exercise you can be your own pianist.

An important feature of exercise 1.4 is the transformation of a vertical sonority into a sung melody. One of the striking characteristics of the twentieth-century repertoire is the flexibility with which composers interchange vertical and horizontal space in their harmonic thinking. The sensibility inculcated by this exercise can be applied to earlier music as well, with important perceptual results.

EXERCISE 1.5: From melodies to verticalities

After hearing a melodic idea of three to eight pitches, sing pitches from bottom to top (*not necessarily in temporal order*), then from top to bottom. Some suitable examples are nos. 3, 4, 6, 10 (mm. 1–4), 23 (mm. 1–3), 48, 52, 64, 66 (to first quarter of m. 4), 74, 114, and 120 (mm. 1–4).

This difficult exercise necessitates retaining all the pitches of the melodic idea in memory, and treating them as if they were a simultaneity.

EXERCISE 1.6: Two-part exercises

Two students or class sections sing the two parts of a duet, then exchange parts. Some suitable examples are nos. 120, 121, 125, 138, 142 (to second quarter of m. 4), and 156 (three-part).

In chamber music, coordinating with and responding to another line is crucial. Exercise 1.6 encourages attentiveness and interaction in playing duets.

After the first group of ear training exercises has become a familiar routine, dictation can begin.

EXERCISE 1.7.: Dictation after singing

After a musical example is heard and successfully sung, as in exercise 1.1, notate each phrase element.

Dictation can be practiced separately from singing, as in exercise 1.8:

EXERCISE 1.8: Dictation without singing

Given the first pitch, take a melody in dictation one phrase element at a time. The player of the melody should emphasize pitch relationships between nonsuccessive tones when the tones are a half-step or whole-step apart, exemplifying the spatial adjacency drilled in exercise 1.2. After you feel that you have correctly notated the melody, have your version played side-by-side with the original melody often enough to make any necessary correction. Almost any melodic segment from the first three groups of musical examples can be used for this exercise, not merely the more easily "singable" ones used for the earlier exercises in this chapter.

EXERCISE 1.9: Dictation of verticalities

A simultaneity of two or more pitches is played on the piano; given the lowest pitch, take the simultaneity in dictation. The pianist should play your version side-by-side with the original often enough for any necessary correction to be made.

EXERCISE 1.10: Two-part examples: More advanced work

a) *For player alone:* Play on the piano one part of any example in group 4 (the examples in two parts), and sing the other part. Exchange singing and playing parts. Eventually memorize the example.

b) *With listener:* After mastering exercise 1.10a, perform the example for dictation purposes. Some suitable examples are nos. 120, 121, 122, 130, 138 and 139 (only sing the second violin part, only play the first violin part), and 142. Any example used for exercise 1.6 may also be used here. The examples with three or more voices from group 5 may also be used, with one voice sung and one or more voices played (such as exx. 156 and 172). A fine example is Stravinsky's *Anthem* ("The dove descending breaks the air"). Women can use the soprano and alto parts of the piece for this exercise, men the tenor and bass parts.

These exercises should begin a course of ear training for twentieth-century music. The assumption is that the student will begin to find his or her own path (that is, structuring devices) when working intensively on this body of music. After this "intuitive" start the structuring devices of the following chapters will be integrated without too much difficulty. When the student has proceeded to later chapters the exercises in this chapter should be repeated, using the same examples; the student will by this time have acquired new knowledge and skills.

Progress should be carefully charted. For example, if studying the chapter on trichords leads to a particularly dramatic improvement in dictation, the exercises of the trichord chapter should be practiced with renewed intensity. Conversely, the benefits of extensive work on the "calisthenic" exercises above will be strongly felt in the more analytically oriented studies in later chapters. A familiarity with the music that is induced by memorization, dictation, and singing is as valuable as an intellectual mastery of the concepts that follow.

2 Dyads: Melodic Motion and Harmonic Structure

A solid understanding of the relations between two tones provides a logical beginning for a structured approach to ear training. Both the radicalism and the complexity of twentieth-century musical languages find their origin in these modest relations. Whereas in earlier music diatonic tonality imposes a powerful interpretation on the vertical presentation as well as the horizontal motion of pitches and harmonies, many twentieth-century treatments of the relations between two tones proceed from the bare facts of pitch and pitch class. In Mozart's Sonata in C Major (ill. int.1) the second pitch, by virtue of being a major third from the first, is incorporated into the same harmony. In Schoenberg's *Pierrot lunaire* (ill. int.2) that same relationship cannot be assumed to convey the same structural meaning, but must be demonstrated through relationships of rhythm, contour, and timbre.

The all-important categories of consonance and dissonance have an a priori meaning in the music of the tonal period. But in much twentieth-century music they are articulated only through the context of rhythm, timbre, and contour particular to a given composition. In diatonic tonal usage the qualitative classification of intervals—perfect, major, minor, augmented, diminished—provides information about their degree of stability. In twentieth-century music there is no comparable way to decode meaning a priori. In earlier music modal and diatonic treatments of intervals between notes grow out of their position in the mode or scale. For example, the expression "parallel thirds" has meaning in a tonal context, even though the intervallic space between the notes may be changing from a major third to a minor third. In the example from *Pierrot lunaire,* however, one cannot assume that the "minor third" in the lower line has greater similarity to the major thirds of the upper line than it does to any other interval, and therefore one must rely on the total musical context to create musical parallelisms and associations.

Although tonally centric influences are present in most twentieth-century music, my explicit purpose is to focus not on these forces but rather on the aspects of twentieth-century musical languages that radically depart from the structuring tools of tonal music (modal considerations play a special role in chapter 6). I therefore use numerical names for pitches, pitch classes, and the various types of interval. These names are free of subjective notions of consonance and dissonance.

The distinction between concrete pitch space and abstract pitch class space (see definitions 2.2 and 2.7) is important to all music theory, but particularly to theories of twentieth-century music. This dichotomy can be profitably integrated into music reading before it becomes part of the musician's hearing apparatus. I will first elaborate on the description of pitches and the intervals that relate them, and then treat pitch classes analogously (although for pitch classes the harmonic notion of the dyad will take precedence over the more melodic one of interval).

At this point the concepts underlying our perception of individual pitches and pitch classes must be defined, as well as those underlying our perception of intervals and two-note harmonies.[1]

DEFINITION 2.1: *Dyad*   A dyad is a harmonic unit constituted of two tones.

DEFINITION 2.2: *Pitch*   A pitch is the specific fundamental defined on the staff, as played by instrumentalists and sung by singers. A pitch name yields no information about timbre, dynamics, duration, function, or inflection. It does however define the approximate frequency of a fundamental tone, and therefore its octave placement. If we assign numbers to pitches, middle C (below the treble clef and above the bass clef) can be called 0.[2] Pitches above middle C are given positive numerical values ($+$n) and pitches below middle C negative numerical values ($-$n) according to their distance in half-steps from middle C.

The C on the second leger line above the treble clef (C6) is called $+24$, and the C on the second leger line below the bass clef (C2) is called -24 (ill. 2.1).

0   +24   -24   +12   -12

2.1. Numerical names for pitches

DEFINITION 2.3: *Unordered pitch interval*   Distances between two pitches measured without regard to temporal order are called unordered pitch intervals. An unordered pitch interval is a simple count of the number of half-steps that separate two pitches. It can be computed by subtracting the pitch number of the lower pitch from the pitch number of the upper pitch. An unordered pitch interval can be regarded as a measurement of the distance between two pitches that sound together, or as the measurement of upward or downward motion between two consecutive pitches (treated as if they were sounding together).

For some examples of unordered pitch intervals see ill. 2.2. From now on I will designate unordered pitch intervals with the abbreviation ip(n). Unordered types of interval are indicated with rounded brackets (   ), and ordered types of interval with angled brackets $<$ $>$.

ip(4)   ip(11)   ip(10)   ip(3)   ip(14)

2.2. Unordered pitch intervals: ip(n)

DEFINITION 2.4: *Ordered pitch interval*   An ordered pitch interval refers to the distance between two pitches that are ordered with respect to time. It is similar to an unordered pitch interval, except that upward direction is described by $+$ and downward direction by $-$. The concept of ordered pitch interval is purely melodic. It cannot be applied to a simultaneity, and therefore differs from the concept of unordered pitch interval in that it is not potentially harmonic.

For some examples of ordered pitch intervals see ill. 2.3. Ordered pitch intervals will be abbreviated from now on as ip<+/−n>.

ip<+9> ip<-16> ip<+18> ip<-13> ip<+15>

2.3. Ordered pitch intervals: ip<+/−n>

EXERCISE 2.1: Reading exercise: Pitch intervals (for one)

Using single-line melodies from the musical examples, read off the *unordered* pitch interval succession at MM = 60 for each ip(n); try to increase this to at least MM = 72. A few appropriate examples are nos. 32, 41, 68, 74, 87, 103–05, 110, and 113; but any melodies from the first three groups of musical examples can be used.

A slightly broader concept of interval that can be the basis of significant musical associations is that of pitch interval modulo 12. Modulo 12, abbreviated mod 12, designates a cyclical concept of musical space in which $12 = 0$ (that is, 1 more than 11 is 0, and 5 more than 10 is 3; see also definition 2.5). Whereas pitch space extends upward infinitely, mod 12 space can be symbolized by the face of a clock. As with pitch intervals, there are unordered and ordered forms of this interval type.

DEFINITION 2.5: *Unordered pitch interval mod 12*   The unordered pitch interval mod 12 is a classification of unordered pitch intervals that reduces them to a number between 0 and 11 by subtracting 12 from them as often as necessary.

This reduction process amounts to an assertion of octave equivalence, a familiar principle from tonal theory. According to this principle, for some analytic purposes all pitches with the same name (C, D, and so on) or pitch class number (see definition 2.7) are considered *equivalent*, though *not identical*. Just as a minor third and a minor tenth can be viewed as equivalent in tonal contexts, ip(3), ip(15), ip(27), and ip(39) are all equivalent under the rubric of ip mod 12(3).

As with pitch intervals, rounded brackets will designate the unordered form of the interval and angled brackets the ordered form of the interval; unordered pitch intervals mod 12 will be abbreviated ip mod 12(n). There are eleven possible types of ip mod 12(n), ranging from 1 to 11. Any C and any A *above it* together make up ip mod 12(9). Any C and any E-flat *above it* make up ip mod 12(3). Any C and any F *below it* make up ip mod 12(7). For some examples of ip mod 12(n) see ill. 2.4.

ip mod 12(4)   ip mod 12(6)   ip mod 12(2)   ip mod 12(4)   ip mod 12(4)

2.4. Unordered pitch intervals mod 12: ip mod 12(n)

DEFINITION 2.6: *Ordered pitch interval mod 12*   The ordered pitch interval mod 12 is a category for *ordered* pitch intervals that reduces them to a number less than 12 by subtracting 12 as often as necessary. The original + or − that accompanies every ordered pitch interval is retained in the ordered pitch interval mod 12.

Ordered pitch interval mod 12 will be abbreviated ip mod 12<+/−n>. "C moving down to A" represents ip mod12<−3>, even if the actual distance is fifteen or twenty-seven semitones. Similarly, "C moving up to A" represents ip mod 12<+9> even if the actual distance is twenty-one or thirty-three semitones. For some further examples of ip mod 12<+/−n> see ill. 2.5.

ip mod 12<-9>   ip mod 12<-9>   ip mod 12<+2>   ip mod 12<-2>

2.5. Ordered pitch interval mod 12: ip mod 12<+/−n>

Table 2.1 illustrates the relationship between the four kinds of interval discussed thus far.

TABLE 2.1. Unordered and ordered pitch intervals mod 12 in relation to unordered and ordered pitch intervals

IP MOD 12(3)[a]			
IP MOD 12<+3>	IP(3)	IP(15)	IP MOD 12<−3>
IP<+15>	IP<+3>	IP<−3>	IP<−15>

[a]This table gives only a sample of each ip mod 12(3) and ip mod 12<+/−3>.

EXERCISE 2.2: Reading exercise: Pitch intervals mod 12 (for one)

Using single-line melodies from examples in appendix 1 that include very large leaps, read off (a) the *unordered* pitch interval mod 12 series, and (b) the *ordered* pitch interval mod 12 series at MM = 120 for each interval.

The concept of ip mod 12(n) provides a helpful transition to the abstract concept of pitch class interval that follows.

DEFINITION 2.7: *Pitch class* A pitch class is a numerical name for a category of *pitches* (see definition 2.2) with the same sound, separated by twelve semitones, or separated by any multiple of twelve semitones. There are twelve possible pitch classes, numbered from 0 to 11. Two possible numbering systems can be useful: one where C is called 0, the other where a pitch central to a given piece is 0.

Pitch class is a far more abstract concept than pitch, but it plays a critical role in twentieth-century structures and is an essential ingredient for ear training. There are twelve pitch classes, designated by the numbers 0 to 11. The number 0 refers to all possible Cs, B-sharps, and D-double flats; in other words, enharmonically equivalent pitches are in the same pitch class. The number 11 refers to all possible Bs, C-flats, and A-double sharps. Pitch class is abbreviated as pc. In numerical terms pc 4 is a category containing the pitches $+4$, -8, $+28$, and so on. When listing groups of pitch classes braces $\{\ \ \}$ will be used.

Pitch class and octave equivalence are taken for granted in many familiar areas of tonal theory, for example in French solfège, in the sample naming of "C" without specifying register, in the use of scale degrees, or in the use of roman numerals to name the roots of chords, regardless of inversion or register. The implications of this distinction from pitch are however carried much further in twentieth-century music and its theory than in the tonal literature.

EXERCISE 2.3: Reading exercise: Pitch classes (for one)

With the same pieces as in exercise 2.1 or similar ones, read off the pitch *class* succession at MM = 144 for each note. Disregard the actual musical rhythm, and keep your eye moving steadily across the page. The pitch classes should be named as follows: oh (0), one (1), two (2), three (3), four (4), five (5), six (6), sev (7), eight (8), nine (9), ten (10), and el (11).

One purpose of this exercise is to make the student familiar with a set of solfège syllables suitable to a chromatic environment of twelve pitch classes. By contrast, the diatonic environment of seven pitch classes of earlier music is adequately described by do-re-mi-fa-sol-la-si or a-b-c-d-e-f-g.

EXERCISE 2.4: Singing musical examples with pitch class numbers (for one)

Practice performing with pitch class numbers the singing exercises of the preceding chapter—exercises 1.1 and 1.3–6.

Like pitch intervals, pitch class intervals can be described as unordered or ordered. Although the concept of ordered pitch class interval has great significance in music theory, particularly in describing twelve-tone rows, for ear training purposes we will restrict ourselves to the unordered pitch class interval. Each type of unordered pitch class interval represents the largest family of dyads.

DEFINITION 2.8: *Unordered pitch class interval*   A pitch class interval is the family of two-note harmonic structures formed between two pitch classes. Unordered pitch class intervals can be described as measurements of the smallest pitch distance possible between representatives of two pitch classes. There are six unordered pitch class interval types, numbered i(1–6).

Any two pitch classes may be described as if they were situated within the span of six semitones. Three common names for unordered pitch class interval are *interval class,* two-note *set class,* and *dyad* or *dyad type.* These two-note units are the fundamental units of harmonic construction for twentieth-century music.

DEFINITION 2.9: *Set class*   A set class is a category for sonorities composed of two to ten pitch classes. Its members are related by either transposition or inversion (see definitions 3.2, 3.3, and 3.4). A two-note set class is synonymous with an unordered pitch class interval or interval class.

(For further definition and elaboration of the concept of set class see chapters 4 and 5.)

To understand the nature of *dyads* (two-note set classes) it may be helpful to visualize the twelve pitch classes as the twelve numbers on the face of a clock (with a 0 in place of the 12): we can say that *the unordered pitch class interval measures the shortest possible route between numbers, whether clockwise or counterclockwise.* In ill. 2.6a pitch classes 2 and 10 constitute an unordered

2.6a. Unordered pitch class interval, I(n), for pcs 2 and 10

pitch class interval of 4, because the smallest possible distance between D and B-flat in pitch space is four semitones. (Heard together, they also make up the set class 2-4: "the two-note harmony that exemplifies type 4.") In ill. 2.6b pitch classes 0 and 9 constitute an unordered pitch class interval of 3. Further

2.6b. I(n) for pcs 0 and 9

examples of unordered pitch class intervals are given in ill. 2.6c. *Unordered pitch class intervals can be described as i(n), or as 2-n: that is, as the nth number of a list of two-note set classes.*

2.6c. Other unordered pitch class intervals: i(n)

Like unordered pitch intervals, unordered pitch class intervals—dyadic set classes—are described as if they were simultaneities. The same unordered pitch class interval includes the motion from pitch class 1 to pitch class 2, the motion from pitch class 2 to pitch class 1, and the sonority of pitch classes 1 and 2 sounding simultaneously.

The six unordered pitch class intervals are the most general and most abstract account of the relations between two pitches. Instead of thinking of an unordered pitch class interval as a measurable distance between two notes, it may be more helpful to think of it as a type of sonority, analogous to its "color," or timbre. This coloristic view of the unordered pitch class interval is emphasized by calling it a dyad or two-note set class.

EXERCISE 2.5: Dictation using "dyad melodies"

(a) Listen to each melody until it is memorized; (b) take it in dictation (given the first pitch); (c) have your version played alternately with the original for purposes of comparison.

EXERCISE 2.6: Sight-singing exercise using "dyad melodies" (for one)

The melodies should also be used for sight-singing. The stages suggested for sight-singing are as follows: (a) Read (do not sing) the pitch class numbers of the melody, with C as "oh," disregarding the notated durations and assigning one beat for each note. (b) Read the pitch class numbers of the melody, following the notated durations. (c) Sing the melody very slowly, with pitch class numbers following the notated durations; repeat this stage until the melody is memorized. It is important to master each of these stages before going on to the next.

THE SIX UNORDERED PITCH CLASS INTERVAL (DYAD) TYPES

Note that the caption for each melody designates the relevant dyad type by two names, its i(n) and 2-n, and lists in braces the two pitch classes forming the dyad.

Melody for i(1) = 2-1, {0,1}

Melody for i(1) = 2-1, {0,1}

Melody for i(2) = 2-2, {2,4}

Melody for i(2) = 2-2, {1,3}

Melody for i(3) = 2-3, {4,7}

Melody for i(3) = 2-3, {2,5}

Melody for i(4) = 2-4, {6,10}

Melody for i(4) = 2-4, {3,7}

Melody for i(5) = 2-5, {1,8} = {8,1}

Melody for i(5) = 2-5, {4,9}

Melody for i(6) = 2-6, {4,10} (six possible combinations of pitch classes)

EXERCISE 2.7: Reading exercise: Unordered pitch class intervals (for one)

Using the same examples as in exercise 2.1 or similar ones, read off the unordered interval succession (1–6) at MM = 120 for each i(n).

Be sure to practice these reading exercises until the tempi specified are attained.

EXERCISE 2.8: Hearing dyads

The pianist should announce a given unordered interval type i(n) of two consecutive pitches or a simultaneity. In response, specify ip mod 12<+/−n> (for two consecutive pitches) or ip mod 12(n) (for a two-note simultaneity), as well as ip<+/−n> (for two consecutive pitches) and ip(n) (for a two-note simultaneity; see ill. 2.7). In doing this exercise it is helpful to make a mental index of the possibilities in a given unordered interval type. For i(1), for example, ip mod 12(1) and (11) are the only two ip mod 12 alternatives and ip(1), ip(11), ip(13), ip(23), ip(25), ip(35), ip(37), and ip(47) are the only possible unordered pitch intervals for melodies confined to a four-octave range.

ip mod 12(3)   ip mod 12<-1>

ip(15)   ip<-13>

2.7. Identifying intervals specifically

EXERCISE 2.9: Comparing dyad pairs

Two melodic successions of two notes each are played that represent the same *unordered interval* type i(n). After two or three playings, decide whether these two dyads exemplify (a) the same ordered pitch interval; (b) the same unordered pitch interval; (c) the same ordered pitch interval mod 12; (d) the same unordered pitch interval mod 12; or only (e) the same unordered pitch class interval (see ill. 2.8). This is an important exercise for future purposes of determining the nature and closeness of pitch and pitch class relationships.

2.8. Relations of pairs of dyads

EXERCISE 2.10: Vocal completion of dyads

After hearing a pitch, sing the pitch that completes an example of a given unordered (pitch class) interval. This completion can be accomplished with two different pitch classes, except for i(6), and several different pitches. Given pitch class D, pc 2, and the request to complete i(3), correct responses include F, pc 5, and B, pc 11, sung at any octave.

EXERCISE 2.11: Identify the ip mod 12(n) and i(n)

a) A two-pitch sonority is heard; choose from among the ip mod 12(n) possibilities. These should be presented in the groups listed below, with enough examples to ensure proficiency within each category. These groupings are made simple to clarify the identity of each ip mod 12(n) by limiting the range of alternatives:[3]

Odd-numbered ip mod 12(n)
Group A: ip mod 12(1) and (5)
Group B: ip mod 12(1) and (3)
Group C: ip mod 12(3) and (5)
Group D: ip mod 12(1), (3), and (5)

Even-numbered ip mod 12(n)
Group A: ip mod 12(2) and (4)
Group B: ip mod 12(2) and (6)
Group C: ip mod 12(4) and (6)
Group D: ip mod 12(2), (4), and (6)

Threefold choices of ip mod 12(n)

Odd-numbered ip mod 12(n)
Group A: ip mod 12(1), (5), and (11)
Group B: ip mod 12(1), (5), and (7)
Group C: ip mod 12(1), (5), (7), and (11)
Group D: ip mod 12(1), (3), and (11)
Group E: ip mod 12(1), (9), and (11)
Group F: ip mod 12(3), (9), and (11)
Group G: ip mod 12(3), (7), and (11)
Group H: ip mod 12(7), (9), and (11)
Group I: ip mod 12(3), (7), (9), and (11)
Group J: ip mod 12(3), (5), (7), and (11)

Even-numbered ip mod 12(n)
Group A: ip mod 12(2), (6), and (10)
Group B: ip mod 12(2), (4), and (10)
Group C: ip mod 12(2), (8), and (10)
Group D: ip mod 12(4), (6), and (10)
Group E: ip mod 12(4), (8), and (10)
Group F: ip mod 12(6), (8), and (10)
Group G: ip mod 12(2), (4), (6), (8),
            and (10)

b) Similar exercises should also be performed on i(n) using the following range of choices:

Odd-numbered intervals
Group A: i(1) and (5)
Group B: i(1) and (3)
Group C: i(3) and (5)
Group D: i(1), (3), and (5)

Even-numbered intervals
Group A: i(2) and (4)
Group B: i(2) and (6)
Group C: i(4) and (6)
Group D: i(2), (4), and (6)

Odd- and even-numbered intervals mixed
Group A: i(1) and (2)
Group B: i(2) and (3)
Group C: i(3) and (5)
Group D: i(4) and (5)
Group E: i(1) and (4)
Group F: i(2) and (5)
Group G: i(3) and (6)

EXERCISE 2.12: Identify the i(n)

Without the benefit of multiple choice, identify the unordered (pitch class) interval type i(n): (1–6) that characterizes simultaneities or two-note successions.

EXERCISE 2.13: Identify the ip(n)

Listen to a simultaneity or two-note succession and identify the unordered pitch interval ip(n) that characterizes simultaneities or two-note successions.

EXERCISE 2.14: Keyboard improvisation (for one)

Using the twofold choices of the earlier exercises, generate dyad progressions in two voices, limiting both the vertical (pc) interval type and the horizontal pitch interval. For example, start with C and F: each voice may move a distance of either ip(1) or ip(2) horizontally without crossing, and must produce i(1) or i(5) vertically, as in ill. 2.9. Parallel motion between voices should be avoided. There are more options if the vertical choices are closer together, as for example with i(3) and i(4). The horizontal limitation to ip(1) and ip(2) should be maintained for all dyad improvisations. Play a series of four sonorities using these rules and repeat them from memory as often as needed. Generate as many examples as you can, using the possible i(n) pairs from the earlier dyad identification exercises and keeping the same horizontal rules.

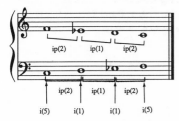

2.9. Model for keyboard improvisations

EXERCISE 2.15: Improvisation used for dictation

Take in dictation the series of dyads generated in the keyboard improvisation, having been told the names of the two initial pitches, the rules of horizontal motion, and the vertical constraints. This exercise will help to demonstrate the integration of horizontal and vertical space so important to composers as disparate as Schoenberg and Stravinsky. In a more difficult version of this exercise, you are not told which i(n) pairs are used for the vertical sonorities. The same improvisation should be undertaken with all interval pairs used in the earlier dyad identification exercises. Later the improvisation should include as many as six sonorities.

EXERCISE 2.16: Identifying intervals between contour extremes in the musical examples

A melody is played from the first three groups of musical examples. Identify the unordered pitch interval ip(n) at extremes of each contour change in any melodic segment of the musical examples. Find the intervals in question as follows: when the melody moves in an upward direction measure from the lowest pitch to the highest (that is, the point where the melody changes direction and begins moving downward); when the melody moves in a downward direction measure from the highest pitch to the lowest (the point where the melody changes direction and begins moving upward; see ill. 2.10). Some particularly appropriate examples are nos. 11, 23, 72, 74, 102, and 109.

2.10. Pitch intervals: ip<n> between contour extremes

EXERCISE 2.17: Identify i(n) series in the musical examples

Listen to a melody, then write down the series of *unordered* intervals (see ill. 2.11). Some appropriate examples are nos. 52, 72, 74, 102, 109, 110, 111 and 112, 114, 130 (parts separately), and 138 (parts separately). Also write vertical ip series.

2.11. Series of *unordered* intervals for a melody: <(1,4,2,6,2)>

EXERCISE 2.18: Identify the i(n) types of verticalities

Listen to either ex. 138 or ex. 139: there are two phrase elements. What are the i(n) types formed by the verticalities in the example? Do the same exercise with any series of two-part simultaneities.

Before attempting the exercises in chapter 4, it is important to feel comfortable with the exercises in this chapter and to review those in chapter 1.

3 Processes: Pitch, Pitch Class, and Contour Relations

In grappling with twentieth-century music we cannot confine ourselves to the definition of musical *structures,* such as interval types or set classes. It is equally important to perceive a range of *relations,* or transformations, that can connect different structures. Relations of this sort can be conceptualized as operations or processes, three of which are retrogression, transposition, and inversion. These processes treat musical elements as combinations either of pitches or of pitch classes.

DEFINITION 3.1: *Retrograde*   The retrograde of a succession of pitches or pitch classes is its temporal order reversal. The retrograde of the pitches $<+6,-5>$ is $<-5,+6>$; the retrograde of the pitch classes $<2,10>$ is $<10,2>$. The arch form consisting of a musical idea followed by its retrograde is called a *palindrome,* an important kind of symmetry in twentieth-century music. Retrogrades can be either reinforced or undercut by the durational pattern and registral placement of their elements (see the examples in ill. 3.1).

3.1a. Retrograde supported by musical context

3.1b. Retrograde undercut by musical context

EXERCISE 3.1: Generating retrogrades

After singing each of the "dyad melodies" on pp. 16-17, sing its retrograde. Follow the guidelines regarding sight-singing that precede these melodies in exercise 2.6.

EXERCISE 3.2: Retrogrades by ear

In response to hearing any of the "dyad melodies" of chapter 2 or a fragment of one of the melodies, sing the retrograde of the melody or fragment. More advanced students can do this exercise with the trichord melodies of chapter 4, the tetrachord melodies of chapter 5, or the musical examples.

DEFINITION 3.2: *Transposition*   Transposition is the addition of a constant interval to a group of pitches or pitch classes.

a) We define the operation $T_{+/-n}^P$ as *pitch transposition* by n half-steps; if n is understood as the number of semitones then $+n$ indicates upward transposition and $-n$ downward transposition. The operation T_{+6}^P (pitch transposition up six half-steps) on the pitch $+2$ gives the pitch $+8$. The operation T_{-7}^P on the pitch dyad $\{+5, +9\}$ results in the pitch dyad $\{-2, +2\}$ (see ill. 3.2).

b) We define the operation T_n as *pitch class transposition* by n where n is greater than or equal to 1 and less than or equal to 11. In pitch class space + and − have no meaning. The operation T_4 (pitch class transposition by 4) on the pitch class 5 results in the pitch class 9. The operation T_5 on the pitch class dyad {3,6} results in the pitch class dyad {8,11}. Because of the modulo 12 nature of pitch class space (see definition 2.7), the operation T_9 on the pitch class dyad {9,11} results in the pitch class dyad {6,8}.

Pitch transposition can be understood to be a special case of pitch class transposition. Unlike pitch class transposition, pitch transposition necessarily retains the pitch interval's size and contour. Examples of pitch transposition and pitch class transposition can be seen in ill. 3.2.

3.2a. Pitch transposition

3.2b. Pitch class transposition
(*not* pitch transposition)

EXERCISE 3.3: Generating transpositions

After singing the "dyad melodies" on pp. 16-17, practice singing transpositions of both their tones and pitch class numbers. In performing the transposition follow the suggested stages for sight-singing in chapter 2. Also practice transpositions of the "dyad melodies" on instruments.

EXERCISE 3.4: Transpositions by ear

A phrase element of four to six tones from the musical examples or one of the "dyad melodies" should be sung, with pitch class numbers used as solfège syllables. Respond by vocally transposing the example, moving both the tones and pitch class numbers a specified distance (see ills. 3.3a, 3.3b). Advanced students can perform this exercise using the trichord melodies of chapter 4, the tetrachord melodies of chapter 5, or the musical examples.

3.3a. Melody for transposition, {4,7}

3.3b. Transposed melody {0,9} =
{9,0} = T_5 of ill. 3.3a

These exercises are crucial for hearing the structural relations between the tones of the example, as well as for acquiring skill in performing the operation of transposition.

DEFINITION 3.3: *Pitch inversion*   Pitch inversion is the mirroring of a pitch or pitches about an axial pitch—a center of inversion in pitch space. To invert a pitch about a given axis, measure the distance of that pitch from the axis and find the corresponding pitch the same distance away from the axis in the opposite direction. Pitch inversion produces symmetrical structures. We define inversion of a pitch about axis 0 as subtraction of that pitch from 0.

We define $I_{+/-n}^{P}$ as pitch inversion where the sum of each pitch and its inversion is $+/-n$. The axis will be found to be $\frac{(+/-n)}{2}$. We call the sum $+/-n$ the *index number*.

In ill. 3.4a (presuming that middle C = 0), given the pitch $+4$ and the axis $+3$, the inverted pitch is $+2$, which is the only pitch the same distance from the axis, $+3$, as is the original pitch, $+4$. This process would be called I_{+6}^{P}; the sum of each pair of original and inverted pitches is $+6$, and the axis is $\frac{+6}{2}$ (= $+3$). In ill. 3.4b, given the pitch $+2$ and the axis 0, the inverted pitch is -2: I_{0}^{P}. In ill. 3.4c, given the dyad $\{+6,-1\}$ and the axis 0, the inversion of the two pitches is $\{-6,+1\}$: I_{0}^{P}. In ill. 3.4d, given the dyad $\{+18,-5\}$ and the axis $+6$, the inversion is $\{-6,+17\}$: I_{+12}^{P}.

3.4a. Pitch + 4 inversion about axis + 3 = pitch + 2

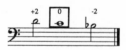

3.4b. Pitch + 2 inversion about axis 0 = pitch − 2

3.4c. Pitch dyad {+ 6, − 1} inversion about axis 0 = pitch dyad {− 6, + 1}

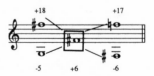

3.4d. Pitch dyad {+ 18, − 5} inversion about axis + 6 = pitch dyad {− 6, + 17}

EXERCISE 3.5: Writing pitch inversions

Using melodies from the musical examples, write out the following pitch inversions: I_{-3}^{P}, I_{+8}^{P}, I_{+13}^{P}.[1]

EXERCISE 3.6: Generating pitch inversions

Practice singing and playing pitch inversions of the dyad melodies of chapter 2. Use several different axes of inversion (see ills. 3.5a–c). Follow the suggested stages for sight-singing in chapter 2, and also practice this process on any instrument. Note that the contour of the inverted melody is the inversion of the original.

3.5a. Dyad melody

3.5b. I_{+16}^{P} of dyad melody of ill. 3.5a

3.5c. I_{+24}^{P} of dyad melody of ill. 3.5a

EXERCISE 3.7: Pitch inversion by ear

A phrase from the dyad melodies should be sung with pitch class numbers. In response sing or play in pitch inversion, using the first tone of the melody as the axis. Advanced students can perform this exercise using the trichord melodies of chapter 4, the tetrachord melodies of chapter 5, or the musical examples.

DEFINITION 3.4: *Pitch class inversion* Pitch class inversion mirrors *pitch classes* about a pair of pitch class axes. The procedure follows that of pitch inversion, except that pitch classes are used instead of pitches. We define pitch class inversion of pitch class n about axis 0 as 12 – n.

We define I_n as pitch class inversion where the sum of each pitch class and its inversion is n mod 12. The sum of the pitch classes 7 and 9 is $16 - 12 = 4$. In this context one axis is $\frac{n}{2}$ ($= \frac{16}{2} = 8$). As with pitch inversion, the sum n is called the index number.

It is essential to understand that under pitch class inversion, two axes are actually present. This results from the circular nature of pc space (note the clock analogy), which means there is a second axis i(6) in addition to that already given. In pc inversions we therefore will always encounter two axes separated by i(6). *The transformation I_n will be about two axes: $\frac{n}{2}$ and $\frac{n}{2} + 6$* (*mod 12*).

In ill. 3.6a, given pc 4 and the axis 3, the inverted pc is 2. The other axis for the pcs 4 and 2 that yields the same result is 9 (see ill. 3.6b). Given the pc dyad {4,10} and the axis 5, the inverted pcs are 6 and 0 (see ill. 3.6c). If the axis is 11 the inverted pitch classes are the same (see ill. 3.6d).

3.6a. Pitch class inversion about
axis 3 = pitch class 2

3.6b. Pitch class 4 inverted about
axis 9 = pitch class 2

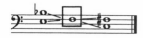

3.6c. Pitch class dyad {4,10} inverted
about axis 5 = pcs {6,0}

3.6d. Pitch class dyad {4,10} inverted
about axis 11 = pcs {6,0}

Although a straight line is the only useful symbol for pitch inversion, the clock is helpful in conceiving of pitch class inversion. The pitch class and its inversion must be equidistant from the axis. Not only are 9 o'clock and 11 o'clock equidistant from the axis 10 o'clock, but they are also equidistant from 4 o'clock.

Because of the abstract nature of pitch class inversion, the concept of *sum* (sometimes called *index number*) can be a more useful concept than *axis* in describing inversionally related pitch classes. Pcs 2 and 6 are inversionally related in a sum 8 situation, which also relates pcs 0 and 8 and pcs 1 and 7. Just as transposition can be conceived arithmetically as the *difference* between pitches related by transposition, inversion can be conceived as the *sum* of pitch classes related by inversion.

The axis about which two odd- or two even-numbered pitches can be related by inversion is a single pitch. The axis around which one odd- and one even-numbered pitch are inverted is made up of two pitches. It also can be thought of as the "crack" between these two pitches. The axis for pitches +4 and +8 is +6, but the axis for +5 and +10 is {+7/+8} or $+7\frac{1}{2}$ (see ill. 3.7a).

In addition, for pc inversions, whereas until now we have conceived of the axis as $\frac{n}{2}$ and $\frac{n}{2+6}$ (mod 12), $\frac{n}{2}$ may lie in the "crack" between two pitch classes. In such a case both pcs form the axis as a pair; the second pair of axes is again found at the distance i(6). And again the concept of sum proves useful in dealing with pitch *class* inversion: in ill. 3.7b, pcs 5 and 8 are inversionally related in a sum 13 (= 1) situation, which also relates pcs 6 and 7, 1 and 0, 3 and 10, and so on. In this case the axes are $\frac{1}{2}$ and $6\frac{1}{2}$. The two pairs of axes are the cracks between pcs 0 and 1 and pcs 6 and 7.

3.7a. Pitch + 5 inverted about axis + 7/+ 8 = pitch + 10

3.7b. Pitch class 5 inverted in a sum 1 situation = pc 8

EXERCISE 3.8: Improvisation and recognition exercise for two or more

A performer should think of an axis about which he or she plays a pair of pitches (related by *pitch* inversion). The listener(s) should sing the axis pitch for each pair.

EXERCISE 3.9: Singing pitch class inversions

Practice singing and playing *pitch class* inversions of the dyad melodies that are *not* pitch inversions. Emphasize maintaining a constant sum between the pitch classes of the original dyad melody and the pitch classes of the inversion. Advanced students can perform this exercise using the trichord melodies of chapter 4, the tetrachord melodies of chapter 5, or the musical examples.

EXERCISE 3.10: Performing processes on musical examples

Example 54 is heard in different types of transposition and inversion. These should be played on the piano both *consecutively*, and *simultaneously* with the original on the piano. Identify the operations that generate these other forms of the music. Do the same with exx. 114 and 74.

EXERCISE 3.11: Improvisation

The most profitable way to improve one's recognition and understanding of process is by improvising. Working at the piano keyboard is the most flexible way to deal with simultaneities, but all processes can also be demonstrated by using melodic instruments. Take any melodic excerpt from the exercises and practice the processes of transposition, retrograde, inversion, and combinations of these.

EXERCISE 3.12: Processes and dyad pairs

Given the possibilities of pitch or pitch class retrograde, transposition, and inversion, two pairs of ordered dyads should be played that exemplify these processes. In response, specify which process is being used. For purposes of practice, the player should begin with pitch processes only. When these are mastered, examples of pitch class processes that are not pitch processes should be added. (A pitch class transposition may or may not be a pitch transposition.) In dealing with inversion the player should first limit the drill to I_0 (that is, inversions with axis 0, and therefore sum 0), then exchange other index numbers with 0.

DEFINITION 3.5: *Invariance* We define invariance as the common element(s) between musical units related by a process such as transposition or inversion. The untransposed pitch retrograde of a musical element maintains its pitch content, but this is a trivial form of invariance. More significant is the choice of a level of transposition or inversion that holds pitch or pitch class as a constant, thus offering the potential for prolonging these pitches or pitch classes while still transforming them.

The first type of invariance occurs in the inversion of a dyad when the two pitches or pitch classes are *mapped onto each other*. Mapping describes the relation between parallel elements in two structures related by a transformation such as transposition or inversion. If {F-D} is such a structure, and T_5 transforms it into {B-flat–G}, we say that F is mapped onto B-flat, and D is mapped onto G. Similarly, if {F-D} is a musical structure, an inversion that maps F onto D necessarily maps D onto F to maintain a constant sum (see ill. 3.8a). If F is assigned pc number 0, then D has pc number 9, and the inversion that maintains pitch class invariance of this dyad is I_9, *that is, the inversion sum 9.* An analogous process can be used for any succession of two pitch classes (see ill. 3.8). Try to avoid the confusion of seeing these examples as retrogrades, which they resemble. Although dyadic invariance through inversion always produces retrogrades, this is often *not* so with larger sets of pitches and pitch classes. The principles introduced here will therefore yield more interesting results when applied in later chapters.

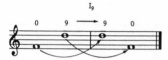

3.8a. Dyadic invariance under I_9

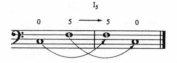

3.8b. Dyadic invariance under I_5

3.8c. Dyadic invariance under I_6

The transformation of two pitch classes related by i(6) offers special possibilities for invariance. It is possible to map onto each other the two pitch classes of such a dyad, just as with any other type of dyad (see ill. 3.8c). But the inversion that *maps each pitch class onto itself* is uniquely available for two pitch classes that constitute an i(6) (see ill. 3.9a). If we transform {F-B}, or {5-11}, by I_{10}, the result is {5-11}, or {F-B}. If we transform {E-flat–A}, or {3-9}, by I_6 (see ill. 3.9b), the result is {3-9}, or {E-flat–A}, because the sum of the mapped pairs of pitches is 6. Although these relations may well seem trivial ones that exemplify identity rather than true transformation, their significance is more apparent when a three-element unit (trichord) *including* i(6) is transformed by the operation I_0. For example, if the original unit is {C-sharp–C–F-sharp}, or {1-0-6}, the operation I_0 produces {B–C–F-sharp}, or {11-0-6}, a *trichord with two invariant elements* under the operation I_0 (see ill. 3.9c).

3.9a. Dyadic invariance under I_{10}

3.9b. Dyadic invariance under I_6

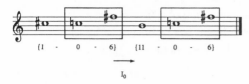

3.9c. Dyadic invariance *within a trichord* under I_0

The other process that maintains pitch class invariance in a dyad comprising i(6) is *transposition by 6*. If we transform {A–E-flat}, or {9-3}, by T_6, the result is {E-flat–A}, or {3-9} (see ill. 3.10).

3.10. T_6 invariance in an i(6) dyad

To summarize, dyadic invariance can be maintained through an inversion in which the two pitch classes are mapped *onto each other*. In the case of two pitch classes related by i(6), invariance can be maintained by two other processes as well: the inversion by which the pitch classes are mapped *onto themselves,* and the *transposition by 6* (T_6). Rahn calls the number of operations on a melodic or harmonic unit that result in invariance the *degrees of symmetry* of that unit.[2]

EXERCISE 3.13: Dyadic invariance

After hearing a melodic dyad, sing the dyad resulting from any operation that maintains pitch class invariance. Do not be put off by the simplicity of this exercise.

EXERCISE 3.14: Process identification

Two melodic dyads are played demonstrating an operation that maintains pitch class invariance. In response, deduce which operation has been heard.

EXERCISE 3.15: Exercises involving musical examples for two or more

Listen to two segments from the musical examples below: (a) and (b). What process has transformed (a) into (b)? Some suitable examples are nos. 134 (mm. 1–2), 138–39, 111, and 112.

For further treatment of invariance in the musical examples see appendix 2, parts 1–3.

An initial step in the structuring process through which twentieth-century music becomes more accessible to memory and understanding can be taken if we suspend our obsession with exact intervals between pitches and pitch classes and instead focus on the contour of the line: its ups and downs. There are two justifications for dealing with contour independently from pitch class: composers have used the identity of a contour and its transformations as a basis for relating musical units; and in terms of pedagogy, the hearing of contour relationships can be an intermediary step to the hearing of pitch relationships.

Pitch relationships can be subdivided into pitch class relationships such as pitch class inversion or pitch class transposition (which exclude contour as a variable) and contour relationships (which exclude pitch class as a variable).

The combinations of contour identity with pitch class inversion or of contour inversion and pitch class equivalence indicate a rich range of structural associations and affects available to twentieth-century composers. The hearing and analysis of contour provides a way of describing *relative* positions and values of pitches rather than the *absolutes* indicated by pitch and pitch class.[3]

I have devised two tools that can be useful in describing contour: the *Contour Adjacency Series* (or CAS) and the *Contour Class* (or CC).

DEFINITION 3.6: *The contour adjacency series* The CAS is an ordered series of + and − signs corresponding to the ups and downs of a melodic line.

The opening theme of the Waltz from Schoenberg's Five Pieces, op. 23 (ill.

3.11), would be described as CAS $<+,+,-,-,+,+,->$. (According to our usage, angled brackets denote an ordered series of elements.)

CAS<+, +, -, -, +, +, ->

CC<1 - 4 - 5 - 3 - 0 - 2 - 7 - 6>

3.11. Schoenberg: Five Piano Pieces, op. 23, no. 5, Waltz

DEFINITION 3.7: *CAS inversion* The inversion of a CAS is the inversion of its + and − signs. Thus CAS $<+,+,-,-,+,-,->$ inverted is CAS $<-,-,+,+,-,+,+>$.

EXERCISE 3.16: Contour processes

a) **Sing or play pitch class *transpositions* of the dyad melodies that are CAS (*Contour Adjacency Series*) *inversions* of those melodies.**

b) **Sing or play pitch class inversions of the dyad melodies that have the same CAS as the original melodies.**

EXERCISE 3.17: Processes: Contour + pc

Sing or play one of the dyad melodies as written, then perform a pitch class transposition or inversion that either has the same CAS or is a CAS inversion.

The second tool for describing contour, more specific than the CAS but still far short of perceiving pitches exactly, is the Contour Class (CC).

DEFINITION 3.8: *Contour class* The CC is an ordered account of the pitches of a musical unit in which the lowest-sounding pitch is 0, the second-lowest is 1, the next-lowest is 2, and so on, and the highest is n − 1 (where n = the number of different pitches in the musical unit). For the waltz theme of ill. 3.11 the CC is <1-4-5-3-0-2-7-6>.

The requirements for membership in a CC family are far stricter than those for membership in a CAS family, because the CC indicates the contour relations of *all* two-note combinations in a unit, whereas the CAS dictates only the relationships between *consecutive* two-note combinations. For purposes of analysis, a CC relationship between units of three notes or more is therefore a special case of the corresponding CAS relationship, as well as a much closer relationship than it. It goes without saying that CAS identity or inversion is implied by CC identity or inversion.

The distance between elements of a Contour Class is called a *contour interval*. The Contour Interval Series (CIS) for the CC <1-4-5-3-0-2-7-6> is therefore <+3,+1,−2,−3,+2,+5,−1>. The concept of Contour Interval is sharply contrasting to that of pitch or pitch class interval, because recognition of it depends on knowledge of the length and Contour Class of the musical unit, and because it is a *relative* description of the space between elements of a Contour Class, not the *absolute* space described by pitch or pitch class interval. A large contour interval has many pitches between those that constitute its boundaries. It may indicate a sense of tension, of space yet to be filled, without necessarily being a large pitch interval as in ill. 3.12. Conversely, a small contour interval does not necessarily designate a small pitch interval.

3.12. Contour interval series

In identifying the CC of a musical unit, the listener must aurally retain at least an approximation of all the pitches of the unit so that they can be spatially ordered. Like Contour Class, Contour Interval is a concept that has real meaning only after the listener has determined what the musical unit is; it therefore depends on a complete, crystallized picture of that unit in musical space. In listening to the music of ill. 3.11, one cannot know the role of A in the CC of the first six pitches without knowing the role of G and F-sharp. Of the CC transformations, inversion is aurally the most accessible.

DEFINITION 3.9: *Contour class inversion* Inversion of a CC, the making of its mirror image, is accomplished by mapping each contour element onto its opposite: the highest CC element is inverted into 0, the lowest into n − 1, the second-highest into 1, and so on. A CC can be inverted by mapping each element so that n − 1 is considered the *index number* for the CC of any musical unit (see the explanation under definition 3.4). Inversions are calculated so that the sum of any contour element and its inversion is equal to the index number of the musical unit. Thus for the Waltz CC, 7 is the index number. Consequently 6 is the inversion of 1, 3 the inversion of 4, and 2 the inversion of 5. The inversion of CC <1-4-5-3-0-2-7-6> is CC <6-3-2-4-7-5-0-1>.

Although some of the processes transforming a CAS are quite easily heard, the comparable transformations affecting a CC are far more elusive, and the identity of a CC may be the only relationship that can really be mastered. But improvisation that uses all the relationships of both CAS and CC can be most helpful in freeing the ear from the tyranny of exact pitch and pitch class associations. The same hearing framework that uses the CC is useful in perceiving modes, and modal transformations often have at their root the identity of a contour class, as in the transformations of the theme from Bartók's Music for Strings, Percussion, and Celesta. The excerpts from this work in the musical examples contain numerous occurrences of contour class equivalence.

EXERCISE 3.18: Contour exercises (for one)

Improvise melodic units with the following CAS designations: $<+,-,-,+>$, $<+,-,-,->$. Improvise the CAS inversion. Generate other CAS forms, eventually increasing the length of the musical unit.

EXERCISE 3.19: Contour improvisation for two or more

a) Improvise a melodic idea with CC $<1-0-4-3-2>$. Listeners should vocally match the CC without attempting to match either the pitches or the pitch intervals. Do the same with CC $<0-4-3-1-2>$. Listeners should perform the inversions of both CCs. Extend this to other CC forms of increasing length.

b) Play two different CC forms that have the same CAS, starting with CAS $<+,->$. Listeners should identify the CCs. Gradually expand the length of the CAS. Be sure that a broad variety of pitch tessitura is used to exemplify the identity of the CAS.

EXERCISE 3.20: Contour exercises with musical examples for two or more

a) A phrase element of any single-line musical example is performed; in response, identify first the CAS, then the CC. Some appropriate examples are nos. 52 and 130 (parts separate).

b) Compare the CAS and CC of ex. 52 with the beginning of ex. 130. Define the relation of cello to violin in ex. 130.

c) In exx. 138 and 139, listen separately to the first violin and second violin parts. Describe the CAS and CC of each phrase element.

d) Listen to ex. 114; write the CC of each four-note unit.

e) Listen to exx. 111 and 112; write the CC of each seven-note unit.

f) Listen to ex. 116; listen separately to each phrase element, identify its CAS and CC, and then do the same for the entire passage.

g) Listen to ex. 75. Divide this first into four three-note units, then into two six-note units. Write the CAS and CC of each, and if possible write the CAS and CC of the entire twelve-note unit.

h) Listen to ex. 109; identify the CAS and CC.

i) Listen to score versions of exx. 175–78; each of the three parts is appropriate for analyzing the CAS and CC.

j) Listen to ex. 110; note the CC for each four-note unit.

k) Example 93 is difficult: listen to the ostinato; identify the CC.

l) In ex. 72 listen to each phrase element, identifying its CAS and CC, then combine the phrase elements until the entire CC can be identified.

m) Do the same for ex. 102 as for ex. 72 in the item immediately preceding.

n) In ex. 122 listen to the left hand alone of mm. 1–3 and 7–9. Compare the CAS and CC of each passage for similarities, contrasts, and relationships.

o) In ex. 54 identify the CC of each phrase element, then compare to exx. 55 and 56.

EXERCISE 3.21: Improvisation using musical examples

While looking at any of the examples above, improvise phrases that exemplify the whole range of contour relationships: first CAS, then CC. Other listeners should identify the relationship, also while looking at the example.

4 *Trichords: Sets of Three Elements*

To describe, understand, and reproduce the music of the tonal period, musicians must be able to manipulate the major and minor scales as the basis of melodic lines, and the triad as the archetypical harmonic unit. In perceiving the interaction of simultaneous lines, the polarity of consonance and dissonance is a critical structuring concept. Although these structures and concepts are relevant to a broad range of twentieth-century literature, many radical changes have displaced them to less absolute roles in musical perception.

These changes include the integration of vertical and horizontal space and the contextualization of the polarity between consonance and dissonance. Only the total musical context, not the preexisting rules of a tonal language alone, can determine which notes appropriately "sound together" (*con-sonans*) and can therefore act as a harmony.

In a post-tonal context the major and minor triads no longer have a priori "superiority" as harmonic units. Together they are merely one of the twelve trichord types, which also include the diminished triad and augmented triad of semiconsonant usage in the tonal period. The theory of twentieth-century music has evolved a tool for describing harmonies independently of any function they may have in a diatonic tonal context: this is the set class (also known as the pitch class set or Tn/TnI set), which gives a general account of the "character" of the harmony based on its unordered pitch class interval content.

DEFINITION 4.1: *Set class*   Set class, first defined in chapter 2, is the fundamental harmonic structure of post-tonal music. The members of a *trichordal* set class have *the same unordered pitch class interval (dyadic) content,* and can be related by the operations of either transposition or inversion. In this book each set class will be defined by two names: (1) its *normal order name* (known elsewhere as the Tn/TnI form), which is discovered through the process of normalization; and (2) its *"Forte number" name,* a two-digit name used commonly in the analytical literature.

In the pages that follow, these and other concepts will be defined and put to use in the context of ear training. The main radical tenet of twentieth-century harmonic language is that *any collection of pitch classes can be structural,* and that no sound is consigned a priori to dissonant status. In pre-twentieth-century music, if we hear the pitches G, C, and D as a simultaneity with G in the bass, tonal practice has us assume that C has an unstable status, and is displacing or delaying the third of a G-major or G-minor triad (B or B-flat; see ill. 4.1).

4.1. Tonal context for {G, C, D}

In tonal theory the entity {G,C,D} is not a harmonic unit with any kind of self-sufficiency, but an unstable entity that implies another, structurally superior entity, namely {G,B,D}. Much twentieth-century music follows this syntax, but the literature we are investigating takes another approach, one in which {G,C,D} is endowed with as much a priori harmonic "value" and self-sufficiency as {G,B,D}. {G,C,D} can act as a *characteristic and central sonority* for a piece, and it can generate structures with as much power as any other collection of three pitch classes. These two facets of {G,C,D} stem from its interval makeup: it contains one instance of i(2), {C,D}, and two instances of i(5), {D,G} and {G,C} (see ill. 4.2).

4.2. Interval structure of {G, C, D}

Before I describe the characteristics of trichordal *pitch class* sets, here is a preliminary exercise that deals with the more concrete world of *pitches and pitch intervals*:

EXERCISE 4.1: Preliminary exercise: Chords in pitch space

A three-note chord or melody is played. First, define the lowest-sounding note as 0, and attempt to notate the other two pitches: for C4, A4, C-sharp5 write <0,+9,+13>. Then take note of the three pitch intervals present: <0,+9> = ip(9), <0,+13> = ip(13), <+9,+13> = ip(4). Finally, assess the unordered pitch class intervals represented by these three pitch intervals: ip(9) = i(3), ip(13) = i(1), ip(4) = i(4) (see ill. 4.3). This extremely important exercise should be drilled intensively and will be referred to later in the chapter.

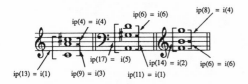

4.3. Pitch interval content for sample trichords

Because of the difficulties most students have in identifying set types by ear, the initial exercises in identifying trichords divide them into three "families," according to conspicuous interval characteristics: *family 1*, three-note sets that include i(1); *family 2*, three-note sets that include i(2) but not i(1); and *family 3*, three-note sets that include neither i(1) nor (2). Illustration 4.4 gives instances of each family of trichordal harmony.

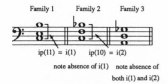

4.4. Families of trichords according to interval content

The assumption underlying this categorization is that i(1) is the most distinctive of the six pitch class interval types, and that its presence or absence in a trichord will be readily apparent. Although i(2) is not as acoustically distinctive as i(1), in the absence of i(1) the presence or absence of i(2) can also be a conspicuous characteristic.

EXERCISE 4.2: Family identification exercise for two or more

Combinations of three pitches are played. Identify the family of each trichord according to its interval content. If you classify the trichord in family 1 sing the two pitches that make up i(1); if you classify the trichord in family 2 sing the two pitches that make up i(2).

Mastering this exercise is an essential step in learning to perceive harmonic types. It can also be a good first step toward the more specific identification of *set classes*.

Another introductory exercise in dealing with trichordal harmonies that falls short of naming the specific set class involves their relationship to superset groups of which I will now define the characteristics (see exercise 4.3).

DEFINITION 4.2: *Superset* A superset of a given set class is a set class containing a larger number of pitch classes than the original set class does. Pitch classes forming the original set class can be found amid the pitch classes forming the superset.

The supersets I have chosen for identifying trichordal subsets are the diatonic collection (and its subset, the pentatonic collection), the whole-tone collection, and the octatonic collection.

DEFINITION 4.3: *The diatonic collection* The diatonic collection is the collection of seven pitch classes represented by the major and natural minor scales and the common medieval modes. One of its twelve transpositions could also be described as the "white-key" set: the seven pitch classes represented by the white keys of the piano.

DEFINITION 4.4: *The pentatonic collection* The pentatonic collection is a collection of five pitch classes familiar from the works of Debussy and Mahler and much Asian music. One of its twelve transpositions could be described as the "black-key" set.

DEFINITION 4.5: *The whole-tone collection* The whole-tone collection is the collection of six pitch classes that can be generated by bringing together six pitches separated by whole-steps, thus dividing the octave into six equal parts. There are two possible transpositions of the whole-tone collection.

DEFINITION 4.6: *The octatonic collection* The octatonic collection can be presented as a scale with eight pitches that fill an octave by alternating whole- and half-steps (see ill. 4.5). It can also be viewed as a combination of any two of the three diminished seventh chords. There are three possible transpositions of the octatonic collection.

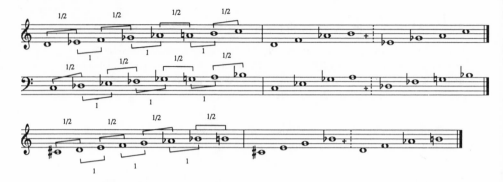

4.5. Octatonic collection

A trichordal set class belongs to a superset group if its pitch classes can be fit into one of the transpositions of that superset. The characteristic quality of the superset can be related to the characteristic quality of its trichordal subsets, as shown in exercise 4.3. A trichord that is a subset of the octatonic mode will be referred to as an "octatonic trichord," a trichord that is a subset of the diatonic mode as a "diatonic trichord," and so on.

EXERCISE 4.3: Singing and listening exercise: Supersets

A trichord within the range of one octave is played. Sing the major, pentatonic, whole-tone, or octatonic scale to which the three notes of the trichord belong, accenting the three pitches of the trichord. Begin on the lowest pitch of the trichord, no matter which scale degree this happens to be.

It should be noted that the presence of i(3), i(6), or both *guarantees membership* in the octatonic superset group. Conversely, the absence of both i(3) and i(6) guarantees that a trichord cannot be in the octatonic superset group. Some trichords belong to both the diatonic and octatonic superset groups, and one trichord type, the "chromatic" trichord, fits into none of these superset groups.

The first step in generalizing a group of unordered pitch classes is to place them in normal order. The purpose of this normalization process, in some ways comparable to detecting the root of a chord in the theory of fundamental bass of the tonal period (but without the structural implications), is to identify the type of harmony, ultimately for purposes of comparison with other harmonies. Although it may seem unnecessarily cumbersome at this point to employ the procedure for normalizing order, or presenting symbols for the pitch classes in most compact form, this procedure will prove useful in determining larger types of families of pitch class sets.

The easiest normalization method for set classes of three elements or more uses the analogy of the clock introduced in chapter 2 to depict two-note set classes. If we want to define the normalized form of a three-note harmony using the pitch classes B-flat, D, and E, the first step is to translate these note names into pitch class numbers, {2,4,10}, and to mark these numbers on the pitch class clock (see ill. 4.6a).

4.6a. E, D, B♭ melody {2,4,10} on the pitch class clock

The second step is to arrange the three pitch classes in *most compact* order. This procedure is somewhat comparable to arranging the notes of a triad to find its root position. Compactness is defined as follows:

DEFINITION 4.7: *Most compact order: Criteria* 1. The most compact order of the pitch classes in a set class has the fewest "hours" between the first pitch class and the last, whether one moves *clockwise or counterclockwise*. If two orderings have the *same* number of "hours" between the first pitch class and the last, and only if they do, the second criterion comes into play:
2. The most compact order has the fewest "hours" between the first and second pitch classes.

TABLE 4.1. Possible consecutive orderings,
clockwise and counterclockwise, for {2,4,10}

Clockwise orderings	Number of "hours" between first and last pitch classes
<2,4,10>	2 clockwise to 10 = 8
<4,10,2>	4 clockwise to 2 = 10
*<10,2,4>	10 clockwise to 4 = 6
Counterclockwise orderings	Number of "hours" between first and last pitch classes
<10,4,2>	10 counterclockwise to 2 = 8
<2,10,4>	2 counterclockwise to 4 = 10
*<4,2,10>	4 counterclockwise to 10 = 6

Given the pitch classes {2,4,10}, it is clear from table 4.1 that the clockwise order for these three pitch classes on the pitch class clock, <10,2,4>, and the counterclockwise order, <4,2,10>, both satisfy the first criterion for compactness. We therefore use the second criterion:

Most compact orders	Number of "hours" between first and second pcs
<10,2,4>	4
*<4,2,10>	2

The *counterclockwise* order <4,2,10> satisfies the second criterion for compactness.

Having found the most compact order, the third step is to *map* the first pitch class of the most compact order onto the symbol [0], and the second and third pitch classes onto symbols that are the appropriate number of hours distant from [0], in this case moving *counterclockwise* (see ill. 4.6b). Because pitch class 4 is mapped onto [0], pitch class 2 is mapped onto [2] and pitch class 10 onto [6].

```
            0
     11          1
6  10              2    2
   9                 3
   8              4    0
     7         5
        6
```

4.6b. Mapping <4,2,10> onto [0,2,6]

DEFINITION 4.8: *Best normal order (name for set class)*   The best normal order name for a set class is a symbolic series derived from the most compact ordering of the pitch classes in that set class. In this symbolic series the first element is called [0], and the other elements are numbered according to their "distance" from the first element. The *best normal order* name for the pitch classes {2,4,10} is symbolized [0,2,6]. In the original melodic fragment of ill. 4.6a we can say that E *plays the role* of [0] in the set class [0,2,6], D plays the role of [2], and B-flat plays the role of [6]. This three-step procedure for defining the *best normal order* name for set classes should be practiced often, as in the following exercise:

EXERCISE 4.4: Finding the best normal order for trichordal
set classes

Find the best normal order name for the following groups of three pitch classes: {A,E,B-flat}, {G,A-flat,C}, {D,E,B}, {B-sharp,E-flat,A}, {C-sharp,F-flat,B}. Create dozens of randomly chosen examples, until you are fluent.

Quick visual recognition of set class types is essential if these are to be
valid tools of musical performance and not merely instruments for analysts.
Reading exercises using the musical examples are the subject of exercise 4.5.

EXERCISE 4.5: Trichord reading exercise (for one)

Use any horizontal line from the musical examples and read off the succession of trichordal
set class names. Two methods should be used: (a) successive trichord types can be read, for
example the notes 1,2,3, then 4,5,6, then 7,8,9; (b) overlapping trichord types can be read,
for example the notes 1,2,3, then 2,3,4, then 3,4,5. These reading drills should be
practiced until musical examples can be read at a tempo of trichord = MM 40. For this
reading exercise it is best if longer melodic passages are used than are provided in the
examples in this book: solo instrumental works such as Berio's *Sequenza for Flute*, the
violin part of Schoenberg's *Phantasy for Violin*, independent string parts of any string
quartets by Bartók, Berg, Webern, Schoenberg, or Stravinsky.

"Trichord reading" must also be practiced using three-part chordal textures, reading
from bottom to top: the piano score of "Eine blasse Wäscherin" (the fourth song from
Schoenberg's *Pierrot lunaire*) is ideal for this purpose.

Eventually, the quality of sound of [0,1,4] or [0,2,6] will be as clear as that of
the major or augmented triad. One aim of this book is to make aural identification of the twelve trichordal set class types an important means of access to the
twentieth-century repertoire. Later in this chapter I give more specific information about the twelve set class types, which will further facilitate identification.

In the context of ear training, we must strive to identify the aural character
of set types as established by their interval content.

DEFINITION 4.9: *Interval vector* The interval vector, a six-digit list of the
frequency of occurrence of each unordered interval type, i(1–6), is Forte's
concise way of listing interval content in set classes of three members or
more (see ill. 4.7). The first digit in the interval vector indicates the number

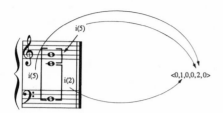

4.7. Interval vector as account of unordered pitch class interval content

of occurrences of unordered pitch class interval (1) in a set of three or more elements, the second digit indicates the number of occurrences of unordered interval (2), and so on. Rahn notates the interval vector as a series of six digits separated by commas and enclosed in angled brackets.[1]

Interval content is unchanged when a group of pitch classes undergoes either inversion or transposition. The trichordal set class type is an extension of the concept of unordered interval. Like the unordered pitch class interval, it is best thought of as a *characterization* of sound rather than as a measurement of distance.

Ideally, reducing a set of three pitches to normal order is a step that can be omitted once we are familiar with the twelve set classes for their sound rather than as artificial intellectual constructs. In later treatments of set classes I use in addition to the best normal order names (which are enclosed in square brackets) a further identifying tag, made up of two integers separated by a hyphen. This is the set class name used by Forte in *The Structure of Atonal Music.*

DEFINITION 4.10: *The "Forte number"*   The "Forte number" for a set class is composed of two digits separated by a hyphen. The first integer specifies the number of different pitch classes in the set class, the second the position of the set class on Forte's list. The advantage that the Forte name has over the normal order name is that it does *not* suggest any real or imagined priority for a pitch arrangement corresponding to the normal order. An understandable pitfall related to using the best normal order name for set classes is that we assign a special significance to the pitch class "playing the role of [0]." As a countermeasure we can identify a trichordal set class through its interval content (as in the interval vector), and then through the two-element Forte number. I will however continue to use the normal order names as well as the Forte numbers, because both conventions are in use in theoretical studies, and because with practice arranging a set in the best normal order is quick and easy. The following list includes the Forte number and normal order name for each of the twelve trichordal set class types:

Forte number	Normal order name
3-1	[0,1,2]
3-2	[0,1,3]
3-3	[0,1,4]
3-4	[0,1,5]
3-5	[0,1,6]
3-6	[0,2,4]
3-7	[0,2,5]
3-8	[0,2,6]
3-9	[0,2,7]
3-10	[0,3,6]
3-11	[0,3,7]
3-12	[0,4,8]

The work in identifying set class types should proceed along two routes: from collection of unordered pitch classes to set class (this route requires fluency in the routines of normalizing); and from hearing of character of sound through interval content to Forte number. The characteristics of an interval family can help to identify set types. With experience, we associate more specific intervallic qualities with specific trichordal set class types, in conjunction with the interval families. For example:

the only set class type that contains *two instances of i(1)* is 3-1-[0,1,2];

the only set class type that contains *two instances of i(2)* is 3-6-[0,2,4];

the only set class type that contains *two instances of i(3)* is 3-10-[0,3,6];

the only set class type that contains *two or more instances of i(4)* is 3-12-[0,4,8];

the only set class type that contains *two instances of i(5)* is 3-9-[0,2,7];

the only set class type in family 1 that contains i(6) is 3-5-[0,1,6];

the only set class type in family 2 that contains i(6) is 3-8-[0,2,6].

To gain a more "intuitive" route to identifying set classes, it is important to work on exercise 4.1 and on its continuation, which follows.

EXERCISE 4.6. Preliminary exercise continued: Interval content of trichords

To define set class types by means of the second route described above, the preliminary exercise on interval content of trichords used earlier in the chapter should be extended by two steps: (a) the three unordered interval types should be put into interval vector form— if we hear a three-note chord the lowest pitch of which we call 0, and that can then be described as $<0,+9,+13>$ with ip(9), (13), and (4) (= i(3), (1), (4)), the interval vector is $<1,0,1,1,0,0>$; and (b) we should learn to identify that interval content with the set type name of 3-3 (and normal order name [0,1,4]).

Most ear training purposes are admirably served if the set class type can be identified without the formalism of interval vectors, but rather by a rundown of interval content: for example, for 3-3-[0,1,4], "one each of i(1), (3), and (4)." Later exercises in this chapter are aimed at improving the student's ability to do this.

In table 4.2 the set 3-3-[0,1,4] is used to demonstrate the hierarchy of unordered pitch class sets: the set class type, its twelve transpositions, and their inversions about axis 0 (I_0), obtainable by subtracting each pc number from 12.

EXERCISE 4.7: Comparing trichord pairs

Two three-note groups that exemplify the same set class type are played. Try to identify the degree and nature of similarity. Are the two trichord pairs made of the same three pitch classes? Are they related by transposition? Or are they related by inversion? This exercise is of the same type as the exercise for dyad pairs (exercise 2.9) and serves a similar purpose in identifying the degree and character of pitch class relationships. Many pairs of each set class type should be attempted when doing this exercise.

Because all the set types above are unordered in both space (or register) and time, we can differentiate members of the *same* set class type by identifying the rip<( )> series of a chord or melody. This involves measuring pitch space rather than the more abstract pitch class space.

DEFINITION 4.11: *Registral pitch interval series*   The rip (registral pitch interval) <( )> series indicates the successive pitch intervals (unordered) of a musical unit from lowest pitch to highest (see ill. 4.8).

4.8. Rip<(p,q)> series: registral pitch intervals of trichords

TABLE 4.2. PC expressions for 3-3-[0,1,4]

3-3-[0,1,4]

{0,	1,	4}	Inv.	{0,	11,	8}
{1,	2,	5}	Inv.	{11,	10,	7}
{2,	3,	6}	Inv.	{10,	9,	6}
{3,	4,	7}	Inv.	{9,	8,	5}
{4,	5,	8}	Inv.	{8,	7,	4}
{5,	6,	9}	Inv.	{7,	6,	3}
{6,	7,	10}	Inv.	{6,	5,	2}
{7,	8,	11}	Inv.	{5,	4,	1}
{8,	9,	0}	Inv.	{4,	3,	0}
{9,	10,	1}	Inv.	{3,	2,	11}
{10,	11,	2}	Inv.	{2,	1,	10}
{11,	0,	3}	Inv.	{1,	0,	9}

EXERCISE 4.8: Rip<( )> recognition exercise

The player announces that a group of sonorities is to comprise representatives of the set type [0,1,4]-3-3, all within a pitch range of two octaves. Make a mental index of the six possible transpositionally related rip<( )> series that could be involved in (0,1,4)— <(1,3)>, <(3,8)>, <(8,1)>, <(4,9)>, <(9,11)>, <(11,4)>, or any of these with a multiple of twelve added to either ip or both. Then identify the heard group of sonorities. This exercise should be done with melodic successions as well as simultaneities.

It is possible to apply the concept of the rip<( )> series to melodies as well as chords, treating them as if they existed only in vertical space (see ill. 4.9). This encourages aural retention of all the notes of a harmonic unit, a desirable goal for any kind of ear training.

4.9. Rip series of melodic fragments

EXERCISE 4.9: Improvisation (for one) and listening exercise

As an adjunct to the original preliminary exercise for recognizing trichords (exercise 4.1), practice transposing and inverting three-note sonorities. (a) After the preliminary exercise is completed, the pianist should transpose it. Identify the "distance," or $T_{+/-n}^{p}$, between the original form of the sonority and its transposed form. (b) By reversing the order of the original rip, you can play an inversion of the original group of pitches (see ill. 4.10). The player should alternate inversions of an original chord with its transpositions, challenging you to identify the relevant transformation.

4.10. Inversion of rip<(p,q)> series

Table 4.3 shows the set class membership in the interval families discussed earlier in this chapter.

TABLE 4.3. Trichordal set classes grouped
according to interval content

Family 1 containing i(1)	Family 2 containing i(2) but not i(1)	Family 3 containing neither i(1) nor i(2)
[0,1,2]-3-1	[0,2,4]-3-6	[0,3,6]-3-10
[0,1,3]-3-2	[0,2,5]-3-7	[0,3,7]-3-11
[0,1,4]-3-3	[0,2,6]-3-8	[0,4,8]-3-12
[0,1,5]-3-4	[0,2,7]-3-9	
[0,1,6]-3-5		

EXERCISE 4.10: Interval family exercises (continued)

Given the interval family of a played trichord, specify which set class it is.

EXERCISE 4.11: Trichord completion

Two tones are played together or perhaps consecutively. Identify the unordered interval type mentally, and then supply vocally the third pitch that will complete an example of a specified trichordal set class type. For example, if the two pitches played are C and F and the specified set class is 3-7-[0,2,5], then sing either D or E-flat: these are the two pitch classes that can complete the trichord of type 3-7-[0,2,5].

In working on this important exercise, one can assume that the set class is defined by its unordered interval content, or that the set class is defined by its best normal order. If we are seeking to complete 3-7-[0,2,5], which can be defined by its interval vector $<0,1,1,0,1,0>$, and we hear C and F, constituting i(5), then we know that a third tone must be supplied that forms i(2) with one of the tones and i(3) with the other. D forms i(2) with C as well as i(3) with F, and thus satisfies these conditions. E-flat forms i(2) with F and i(3) with C, thus also satisfying the conditions. In learning to identify and generate the twelve types of trichord set class, one should practice this exercise often, using both defining characteristics: interval content and best normal order.

EXERCISE 4.12: Set class identification (continued)

Three-note chords and three-note melodic figures are played. Identify the set class. At first the exercise can be limited to each of the three interval families so as to limit the field of choices, but eventually it should be possible to recognize the twelve trichordal set class types. There are two versions of this exercise: the first uses only the most compact pitch representatives of the set classes; the second uses scattered pitch representatives of the set classes.

An important characteristic of musical units and gestures is the presence or absence of inversional symmetry, either within the unit or in the relation of one unit to another.

DEFINITION 4.12: *Inversional symmetry*   A pitch class set can be characterized in two ways as inversionally symmetrical:
a) A pitch class set is inversionally symmetrical if there is a spatial arrangement for it of which the rip<( )> forms a palindrome (it is the same forward and backward). A trichord that *could* have the rip<(3,3)> is an example of an inversionally symmetrical pitch class set type.
b) A pitch class set is inversionally symmetrical if its elements can be inverted in such a way that there is complete pitch class invariance between the original representation of the set and a particular inversion. The pitch class set 3-6-[0,2,4] is inversionally symmetrical, because if $\{0,2,4\}$ is P_0, then its I_4 (inversion sum 4), <4,2,0> = $\{0,2,4\}$, produces complete pitch class invariance. In I_4, 0 is inverted into 4, 2 into 2, and 4 into 0. This process is called *mapping by inversion*. The process I_4, which describes the relations between two potentially different members of the pitch class set [0,2,4]-3-6, can also be described as inversion about the pc axis 2.

Because of their particular intervallic contents, the five inversionally symmetrical trichordal set types are distinguished relatively easily from one another. A list of the inversionally symmetrical trichord types follows:

3-1------[0,1,2]------family 1

3-6------[0,2,4]------family 2
3-9------[0,2,7]------family 2

3-10-----[0,3,6]------family 3
3-12-----[0,4,8]------family 3

Note that 3-9-[0,2,7] is symmetrical by virtue of the possible rip<(7,7)>, even though its normal order name does not immediately suggest its symmetrical character.

EXERCISE 4.13: Listening exercise on symmetry

Two pitches are played. Identify the resultant pitch interval, then add one of the two pitches (either the one above or the one below will produce a similar result) that will make it an inversionally symmetrical trichord, an example of one of the five types. The symmetry should work in pitch space: that is, the rip series should consist of two equal numbers— for example <(13,13)> or <(7,7)>. Other listeners should then identify the trichord type and its rip<( )> series.

EXERCISE 4.14: More on inversional symmetry

The player specifies that the trichord to be heard will be one of the five inversionally symmetrical trichords. Identify which one it is. There are two stages in this exercise: the player announces that the trichord is in pitch symmetrical form, and it is heard as such; and the trichord's symmetry exists only in pitch class space, not in pitch space (see ill. 4.11).

DEFINITION 4.13: *Degree(s) of symmetry*   We can define the degree of symmetry of a set class as the number of transformations that yield complete pitch class invariance. For example, i(6) has two degrees of symmetry *more* than any other dyad type, because *two* different inversional processes as well as transposition leave the pitch class content invariant.

If we invert <D–C–C-sharp>, which we can describe as a <2-0-1> representative of [0,1,2], so that D and C map onto each other and C-sharp maps onto itself (I_2), the result will be <C–D–C-sharp>. The analogous processes are shown in ill. 4.11 for all five inversionally symmetrical trichord types.

4.11a. Trichordal invariance: 3-1-[0,1,2]

4.11b. Trichordal invariance: 3-6-[0,2,4]

4.11c. Trichordal invariance: 3-9-[0,2,7]

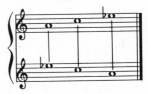

4.11d. Trichordal invariance: 3-10-[0,3,6]

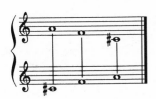

4.11e. Trichordal invariance: 3-12-[0,4,8]

Like the dyad i(6), the trichord 3-12-[0,4,8] is a special case, in that more than one transformative operation can result in pitch class invariance. Not only the inversion I_8 (see ill. 4.11e) but the inversions I_4 and I_0 as well as the transpositions T_4 and T_8 result in complete pitch class invariance for {0,4,8}, a representative of 3-12 (see ill. 4.12). Therefore, 3-12 is characterized by *four*

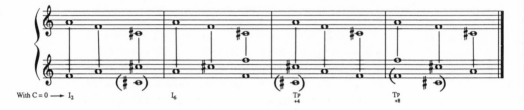

With C = 0 ⟶ I_2 I_6 Tp_{+4} Tp_{+8}

4.12. Additional operations resulting in invariance for 3-12-[0,4,8]

more degrees of symmetry than the other four inversionally symmetrical trichord types. Note that just as i(6) can bisect the octave equally, 3-12 can trisect the octave equally.

EXERCISE 4.15: Singing exercise for two or more: Transformations and invariance

A melodic form of one of the inversionally symmetrical trichord types is played. Sing back a transformation (inversion or transposition) of the melody that demonstrates pitch class invariance.

EXERCISE 4.16: Identifying invariant transformations

A pair of melodic fragments is played that demonstrate invariance under transposition or inversion of one of the symmetrical trichord types. Identify which process has related the two fragments. For further work on inversional symmetry and invariance see appendix 2, parts 1–3.

EXERCISE 4.17: Keyboard improvisation (for one)

a) **Play a keyboard improvisation of trichord types, using arbitrary rules (see ill. 4.13).
   For example: (1) play a member of family 1, then of family 2, then of family 3, never
   moving any of the three voices more than ip(2) and avoiding crossed voices (see ill.
   4.13a); (2) do the same, but always having one common pitch (see ill. 4.13b); (3) do the
   same, but where possible with two common pitches (see ill. 4.13c).**

4.13a. Keyboard improvisation 1

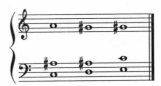

4.13b. Keyboard improvisation 2

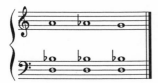

4.13c. Keyboard improvisation 3

4.13d. Keyboard improvisation 4

b) **Use different transpositions and voicings of trichords of the types 3-3-[0,1,4] and 3-7-
   [0,2,5] as a source of verticalities, never moving any voice more than ip(2) (see ill.
   4.13d). Two successive instances of a given set class type are possible in this exercise,
   but parallel motion among all three voices should be avoided. This exercise should be
   repeated often to achieve control of the horizontal and vertical dimensions of three-
   voiced successions.**

EXERCISE 4.18: Continuation of improvisation exercise: Material for dictation

**After the instructor makes up rules for keyboard improvisations, as in exercise 4.17,
either reconstruct the rules for horizontal motion and verticalities from the aural evidence,
or take the chord succession in dictation after the rules for horizontal motion and verticalities have been announced. The pianist should play a four-chord series, then be
required to repeat the series (from memory) as often as necessary for purposes of dictation. The exercise can be simplified in one way if the rules for horizontal motion are left
constant: there should be no motion greater than ip(2).**

Regarding supersets, our first consideration is simply whether a trichord is or is not a diatonic, pentatonic, whole-tone, or octatonic subset. The subset groups are listed below (the diatonic subsets that are also pentatonic subsets are in boldface):

Diatonic subsets	Whole-tone subsets	Octatonic subsets
3-2-[0,1,3]	3-6-[0,2,4]	3-2-[0,1,3]
3-4-[0,1,5]	3-8-[0,2,6]	3-3-[0,1,4]
3-5-[0,1,6]	3-12-[0,4,8]	3-5-[0,1,6]
3-6-[0,2,4]		3-7-[0,2,5]
3-7-[0,2,5]		3-8-[0,2,6]
3-8-[0,2,6]		3-10-[0,3,6]
3-9-[0,2,7]		3-11-[0,3,7]
3-10-[0,3,6]		
3-11-[0,3,7]		

To acquire a greater facility in grouping these subsets and supersets, it is useful to identify subsets according to whether they belong to the diatonic and octatonic supersets: in group 1 are trichordal sets that belong to the diatonic but not to the octatonic superset; in group 2 are trichordal sets that belong to the octatonic but not the diatonic superset; in group 3 are trichordal sets that belong to both the diatonic and the octatonic superset; and in group 4 are trichordal sets that belong neither to the diatonic nor to the octatonic superset. These superset groups are set forth in table 4.4.

TABLE 4.4. Trichordal set classes grouped according to superset membership

Group 1 diatonic only	Group 2 octatonic only	Group 3 both diatonic and octatonic	Group 4 neither diatonic nor octatonic
[0,1,5]-3-4	[0,1,4]-3-3	[0,1,3]-3-2	[0,1,2]-3-1
[0,2,4]-3-6		[0,1,6]-3-5	[0,4,8]-3-12
[0,2,7]-3-9		[0,2,5]-3-7	
		[0,2,6]-3-8	
		[0,3,6]-3-10	
		[0,3,7]-3-11	

EXERCISE 4.19: Superset groups

The pianist performs a three-note chord: identify the group according to table 4.4, then identify the specific trichord type.

Grouping with respect to the two whole-tone scales is helpful to some students. In pitch class sets all pcs with odd numbers belong to one transposition of the whole-tone scale, and all pcs with even numbers belong to the other. In table 4.5 trichord types are divided into those with all three members in one whole-tone scale, and those with two members in one whole-tone scale and one in the other.[2]

TABLE 4.5. Trichordal set classes grouped in whole-tone groups

Whole-tone group 1 (3 + 0)	Whole-tone group 2 (2 + 1)
[0,2,4]-3-6	[0,1,2]-3-1
[0,2,6]-3-8	[0,1,3]-3-2
[0,4,8]-3-12	[0,1,4]-3-3
	[0,1,5]-3-4
	[0,1,6]-3-5
	[0,2,5]-3-7
	[0,2,7]-3-9
	[0,3,6]-3-10
	[0,3,7]-3-11

Hearing through the "whole-tone filter" is by no means a natural skill, or one reinforced through most performing or listening experiences. It is a useful tool for characterizing the harmonies of any number of pitches, and for perceiving harmonies with similarities that might otherwise go unnoticed. It can be practiced by means of the following exercise:

EXERCISE 4.20: Whole-tone membership

A trichord (either melodic or chordal) within the range of one octave is played. Sing the whole-tone scale in both ascending and descending directions that includes *two or three* of the pitches. Accent the pitches of the played trichord while singing the scale (see ill. 4.14).

4.14. "Whole-tone group" singing exercise

In characterizing the twelve trichordal set classes I will indicate the following: the Forte number, the normal order number, the interval vector, whether the set class is inversionally symmetrical, whether fewer than twenty-four unordered pitch class collections belong to the set class (only inversionally symmetrical trichords have fewer than twenty-four distinct pitch class collections by virtue of trichordal invariance), to which family the set class belongs (see table 4.3), to which superset membership group it belongs (see table 4.4), to which whole-tone group it belongs (see table 4.5), and some other important distinguishing characteristics. Note that membership in whole-tone group 1 means that a trichord is a *whole-tone subset*.

EXERCISE 4.21: Trichord melodies: Sight-singing and dictation

After the information about each set class type is given, melodies made up of three pitch classes constituting that set class type are played. Their pitch class content is shown in braces, first in ascending order, then in the "most compact" order that is the basis for the normal order name. These melodies should be used first for dictation, then for sight-singing.

a) In dictation the melody should be heard until it is memorized, then written down. The written melody should then be compared with the original and corrected if necessary.

b) When using the melody for sight-singing, sing it with pitch class numbers (C = 0); then vocally transpose and invert both the tones and numbers to all possible levels (eleven possible transpositions, twelve possible inversions). In singing the melodies as well as in transposing and inverting them, follow the three stages suggested in exercise 2.6 for sight-singing: rhythmless reading, rhythmic reading, slow singing. Transpositions and inversions should be done instrumentally as well as vocally. In cases of transpositionally and inversionally symmetrical trichords, be aware of which levels of inversion and transposition maintain pitch class invariance.

The use of the "trichord melodies" for sight-singing and dictation is meant to establish great familiarity with the sonority and interval content of each trichord type. That is why such extensive information is given about each of the set classes in the following section.

LIST OF TRICHORDS

3-1
[0,1,2]
Inversionally symmetrical
Twelve pitch class collections
Interval vector <2,1,0,0,0,0>
Family 1
Superset group 4
Whole-tone group 2 (2 + 1)
    This trichord is characterized as the "chromatic" trichord, because its most compact pitch representation is a three-note segment of the chromatic series.

Melody for 3-1-[0,1,2]. {0,1,2}

3-2
[0,1,3]
Interval vector <1,1,1,0,0,0>
Family 1
Superset group 3
Whole-tone group 2 (2 + 1)

    This trichord could be characterized as the "octatonic" trichord, because its most compact pitch representations are adjacent segments of the octatonic scale (an alternating series of ip 1 and ip 2).

Melody for 3-2-[0,1,3]. {1,2,4}

Melody for 3-2-[0,1,3]. {2,4,5} = {5,4,2}

3-3
[0,1,4]
Interval vector <1,0,1,1,0,0>
Family 1
Superset group 2
Whole-tone group 2 (2 + 1)

This is one of the most characteristic trichords in early noncentric music—the beginnings of Schoenberg's Piano Piece, op. 11, no. 1, and of Bartók's Music for Strings, Percussion, and Celesta are only two examples. The trichord is a subset of the octatonic scale, and of the ascending "melodic minor" scale (degrees 1, 3, and 7), but not of the traditional modes as expressed in the diatonic set.

Melody for 3-3-[0,1,4]. {3,4,7}

Melody for 3-3-[0,1,4]. {4,7,8} = {8,7,4}

3-4
[0,1,5]
Interval vector <1,0,0,1,1,0>
Family 1
Superset group 1
Whole-tone group 2 (2 + 1)

This trichord is a subset of the diatonic set: scale degrees 3, 4, and 6 of the major scale form this set class, as do scale degrees 1, 3, and 7, scale degrees 1, 3, and 4, and scale degrees 1, 5, and 7.

Melody for 3-4-[0,1,5]. {5,6,10}

Melody for 3-4-[0,1,5]. {6,10,11} = {11,10,6}

3-5
[0,1,6]
Interval vector <1,0,0,0,1,1>
Family 1
Superset group 3
Whole-tone group 2 (2 + 1)

This set type is highly characteristic of Bartók and of the Stravinsky of *Rite of Spring,* even more than would be expected from its occurrence eight times in the octatonic series. The set [0,1,6] also occurs twice in the diatonic set.

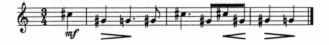

Melody for 3-5-[0,1,6]. {1,7,8} = {7,8,1}

Melody for 3-5-[0,1,6]. {1,2,8} = {2,1,8}

3-6
[0,2,4]
Inversionally symmetrical
Twelve different pitch class collections
Interval vector <0,2,0,1,0,0>
Family 2
Superset group 1
Whole-tone group 1 (3 + 0)

This trichord is highly characteristic of the diatonic set—it occurs three times in it, as the incipit and degrees 4, 5, 6 and 5, 6, 7 of the major scale. But it is even more characteristic of the whole-tone series, because it is the trichordal type for any three consecutive whole-tone scale degrees.

Melody for 3-6-[0,2,4]. {1,9,11} = {9,11,1}

3-7
[0,2,5]
Interval vector <0,1,1,0,1,0>
Family 2
Superset group 3
Whole-tone group 2 (2 + 1)

This trichord occurs in both the octatonic and diatonic sets eight times, but it is most easily identified through its four occurrences in the pentatonic set. Leonard Bernstein called one of its pitch representations a musical linguistic universal used in the "teasing" song. It has found use as a typical turn of phrase both in Western music since the medieval period and in much Asian music.

Melody for 3-7-[0,2,5]. {0,3,10} = {10,0,3}

Melody for 3-7-[0,2,5]. {2,4,11} = {4,2,11}

3-8
[0,2,6]
Interval vector <0,1,0,1,0,1>
Family 2
Superset group 3
Whole-tone group 1 (3 + 0)

This trichord is a subset of the diatonic, octatonic, and whole-tone sets, but the tritone indicates its exclusion from the pentatonic set. One tonal treatment of [0,2,6] is as the root, third, and seventh of an incomplete dominant seventh chord. In "counterclockwise" form, this trichord can be thought of as the root, fifth, and seventh of the half-diminished seventh chord, which is the inversion of the dominant seventh.

Melody for 3-8-[0,2,6]. {0,2,6}

Melody for 3-8-[0,2,6]. {1,5,7} = {7,5,1}

3-9
[0,2,7]
Inversionally symmetrical
Twelve different pitch class collections
Interval vector <0,1,0,0,2,0>
Family 2
Superset group 1
Whole-tone group 2 (2 + 1)

Along with 3-7, this is the most characteristically diatonic (and pentatonic) trichord. It is often heard as a "fourth chord." In tonal contexts it is often heard also as an entity resembling a $\frac{5}{2}$ figured bass, for example as a bass suspension.

Melody for 3-9-[0,2,7]. {2,4,9}

3-10
[0,3,6]
Inversionally symmetrical
Twelve different pitch class collections
Interval vector <0,0,2,0,0,1>
Family 3
Superset group 3
Whole-tone group 2 (2 + 1)

This is the diminished triad of tonal usage. It is both a diatonic and an octatonic subset.

Melody for 3-10-[0,3,6]. {3,6,9}

3-11
[0,3,7]
Interval vector <0,0,1,1,1,0>
Family 3
Superset group 3
Whole-tone group 2 (2 + 1)

This trichord type, well known as the major or minor triad, is a subset of the diatonic, pentatonic, and octatonic sets.

Melody for 3-11-[0,3,7]. {4,7,11}

Melody for 3-11-[0,3,7]. {0,4,9} = {9,0,4}

3-12
[0,4,8]
Inversionally symmetrical
Transpositionally symmetrical
Four different pitch class collections
Interval vector <0,0,0,3,0,0>
Family 3
Superset group 4
Whole-tone group 1 (3 + 0)

The augmented triad is the only trichordal set class that contains only one interval type. It belongs neither to the diatonic nor to the octatonic set, but it does occur three times in the whole-tone set.

Melody for 3-12-[0,4,8]. {2,6,10}

EXERCISE 4.22: Modal singing exercise (for one)

A good way to drill sets of any size is to sing them in a pitch representation corresponding to the best normal order. Then the other rotations of that ordering should be sung: for [0,1,2] the notes C, C-sharp, D, and upper C should be sung in ascending order, then C-sharp, D, C, and upper C-sharp, then D, C, C-sharp, and upper D (see ill. 4.15a). For this exercise the pitch class numbers "oh" to "el" should be used.

The same exercise should be performed in a downward direction, inverting the pitch intervals. Thus the initial version of [0,1,2] starting on C would be C, B, B-flat, and lower C, then B, B-flat, C, and lower B, and so on (see ill. 4.15b).

4.15a. Modal singing exercise for 3-1-[0,1,2]

4.15b. Modal singing exercise: downward form for ill. 4.15a

EXERCISE 4.23: Chordal listening exercise

The three spacings of the modal singing exercise can also be played as simultaneities on the piano. Identify the spacings as *positions 1, 2, and 3* of a given set class.

EXERCISE 4.24: Arpeggio exercise, piano or other instrument (for one)

This is an elaboration of the modal singing exercise for wind and string players, which makes practicing trichord types comparable to practicing instrumental broken chord patterns: play any transposition of a trichord type in a spacing that corresponds to its normal order name, but ending two octaves higher than the starting note. This would be an arpeggio in position 1. If we were dealing with a trichord of the type 3-3-[0,1,4] with C functioning as [0] in position 1, the pattern would unfold as in ill. 4.16a.

4.16a. C as position 1 in [0,1,4]

4.16b. Downward form for ill. 4.16a

If C were functioning as a bass in position 2, it would function as the [1] in the [0,1,4] and the pattern would unfold as in ill. 4.17.

4.17a. C as position 2 in [0,1,4]

4.17b. Downward form for ill. 4.17a

If C were acting as a bass in position 3, it would function as the [4] in [0,1,4] and the pattern would unfold as in ill. 4.18.

4.18a. C as position 3 in [0,1,4]

4.18b. Downward form for ill. 4.18a

The downward form of the arpeggio inverts the upward form, and the whole pattern would end where it started (see ills. 4.16b, 4.17b, and 4.18b).

EXERCISE 4.25: Arpeggio exercise with listener(s)

Listen to exercise 4.24 being performed. Identify the position and set class type.

Another concept of trichords defines them as the result of the division of a pitch interval: any pitch interval greater than ip(1) can have an intervening pitch introduced between its two elements. Two pitches forming ip(5) can have pitches introduced that result in [0,1,5], [0,2,5], [0,2,5], and [0,1,5] (see ill. 4.19).

EXERCISE 4.26: Exercise for two or more: Trichords resulting from partitioning of pitch interval

The player announces that the pitch interval between outer voices of a series of three-note chords is any pitch interval between ip(3) and ip(25). The player then subdivides this pitch interval with one more pitch. Identify which trichordal set class is being presented. Repeat with other pitch intervals (see ill. 4.19).

rip<(1,4)> [0,1,5]   rip<(2,3)> [0,2,5]   rip<(3,2)> [0,2,5]   rip<(4,1)> [0,1,5]

4.19. Trichords resulting from partition of ip(5)

EXERCISE 4.27: Process recognition

It is important to recognize the operations of transposition and inversion as they relate trichords within set classes. To drill this process, sing a series of three pitches (using pitch class numbers) to be labeled P_0, such as <0-2-5>. Then sing T_8 of P, which is the series of pitches eight semitones higher, namely, <8-10-1>. In singing transpositions contour should be preserved, so that these are not merely pitch class transpositions but pitch transpositions.[1]

Inversion about the axis 0 can be performed by subtracting the set of pitch class numbers from 12 to produce an inverted form of the set. As with transposition, sing a series of three pitches (using pitch class numbers) to be labeled P_0, such as <0-2-5> (an upward-moving contour), then sing the inversion, which is <0-10-7> (a downward-moving contour). In singing inversions contour should be inverted, so that the sung results are not just pitch class inversions but pitch inversions. Inversion of the original <0-2-5> about axis 4 can be generated as *inversion sum $8-I_8$*. Using the image of the pc clock, it is easy to see how <0-2-5>, clockwise, is inverted into <8-6-3>, counterclockwise.

The operations through which different representatives of a set class type are related should become as much an aspect of ear training as the recognition of harmonic equivalence. A common problem of atonal theory is posed by the misleading idea that a common set class name makes two entities not merely "equivalent" with respect to their membership in a family, or through an operation, but identical. Transformation is another word for operation, and the sense of movement from one representative of a pitch class set to another is at least as important to the understanding of the music as is the recognition of "equivalence."

DEFINITION 4.14: *Segmentation*   To say that a set class occurs in a musical context means to perform the act of segmentation: to decide that some pitch classes adhere to each other more than they adhere to others either in space or time, or conceivably through differentiation of timbre. The set class identifies those pitch classes as a structural segment of the music.

In tonal music the concepts of consonance and dissonance have an a priori significance: consonances are graded as to stability according to linguistic rules established between the fifteenth century and the eighteenth century, and threatened only by modest ambiguities in the nineteenth century. In much twentieth-century music these linguistic rules are only tenuously applicable, and the context of interior relationships is the only consistently reliable guideline for musically meaningful segmentation. Musical segments are structures delineated by contour, register, rhythm, and set class characteristics.

The melody that opens the Praeludium of Schoenberg's Suite, op. 25, projects the segmentation in ill. 4.20a by repeating the set class 3-5-[0,1,6],

4.20a. Schoenberg segmentation 1

the contour class <1-2-0>, and the rhythmic contour "long-short-medium." The repeated motions by ip<− 1> and finally ip mod 12<− 1> give additional support to this segmentation. The same melody projects the segmentation in ill. 4.20b by repeating set class 3-2-[0,1,3] and the rhythmic and metric motive of two eighth-note upbeats leading to a downbeat attack. A third

4.20b. Schoenberg segmentation 2

segmentation, shown in ill. 4.20c, is achieved by repeated delineation of the
set class 3-3, at first through the domains of durational pattern (units of ⅝) and

4.20c. Schoenberg segmentation 3

registral adjacency, then through articulation of the hemiola. Because these
segmentations are limited to trichords and because the other voices in the
polyphonic texture are not being considered, not all the melodic tones are
included. Nor do they determine the "strongest segmentation" for the passage.
They do, however, give an indication of how the domains of contour, rhythm,
and set class characteristics interact in shaping musical continuity in a post-
tonal idiom.[3]

Analytical ear training that has segmentation of this kind as its goal is best
accomplished with slow, repeated playing of phrase elements from musical
examples, followed by diagramming of set types, contours, and rhythmic
relations. In music with more than one instrument or more than one distinct
type of sonority (for example, pizzicato and arco), timbre is also an important
consideration in segmenting the musical continuity.

EXERCISE 4.28: Exercises with musical examples

a) Listen to ex. 130 (first violin part): compare the rip of mm. 3–4 and 5–6. Then describe the relation of pc sets given that C-sharp = 0.

b) Listen to exx. 175–78. In each segment: (1) identify the set class type of each verticality; (2) enumerate the number of pitches or pitch classes held in common between successive chords and then specify which voice is occupied by the common pitch or pitch classes in successive chords: top, middle, or bottom; (3) identify the relationship between any two chords of the same set class type—pitch or pitch class transposition or inversion. If this is too difficult as a response to hearing the whole musical segment, the pianist should merely play the two chords in succession.

c) Listen to ex. 170 (three voices of the accompaniment). Identify the set class type of each verticality. After hearing phrase elements in pairs, identify the following degrees of similarity between verticalities: pitch identity, pitch class identity, set class type (if it is a pitch or pitch class transposition identify its distance, and if it is an inversion identify the axis for pitch or pitch class inversion). The task can be simplified if the pianist just plays pairs of chords with the same set class type rather than pairs of phrase elements.

d) Listen to ex. 122 (right and left hands separately). Identify the rip<( )> and set class types of each trichordal simultaneity.

e) Listen to ex. 83 (m. 3, right hand). What are the set class types of the two trichords that make up the six sixteenths of the bar? If the six sixteenths are divided spatially instead of temporally, what are the set class types of the "lowest" trichord? Of the highest trichord?

f) Listen to ex. 127 (m. 1). Identify the trichord type within each quarter-note beat.

g) Listen to ex. 9. Identify the rip<(n)> and set class types of all three-note groups with (1) the durational pattern of two sixteenths followed by a long note; and (2) the durational pattern of three consecutive eighth-notes.

5
Tetrachords:
Sets of Four Elements

The aural identification and manipulation of the twenty-nine tetrachordal pc set types is a difficult but achievable goal for performing musicians as well as for theorists and composers. As a first step toward aural identification of each set type we classify them into groups and families based on their interval and subset content, and on their membership in superset groups.

Interval content is expressed in the interval vector of tetrachords in the same way as it is for trichords. For [0,1,2,3]-4-1, if we use the pitch classes {0,1,2,3} the dyads comprise the pitch classes {0,1} (= i(1)); {0,2} (= i(2)); {0,3} (= i(3)); {1,2} (= i(1)); {1,3} (= i(2)); and {2,3} (= i(1)). Among the six dyads present are three instances of i(1), two of i(2), and one of i(3); therefore the interval vector is <3,2,1,0,0,0> (see ill. 5.1).

5.1. Interval content of [0,1,2,3]-4-1

The treatment of tetrachords in interval content families is the same as that of trichords. If a set contains i(1) it is in family 1, if it contains i(2) but not i(1) it is in family 2, and if it contains neither i(1) nor i(2) it is in family 3. This classification system results in the families of tetrachordal set classes shown in table 5.1.

TABLE 5.1. Tetrachordal set classes grouped according to interval content

Family 1 containing i(1)	Family 2 containing i(2) but not i(1)	Family 3 containing neither i(1) nor i(2)
[0,1,2,3]-4-1	[0,2,4,6]-4-21	[0,3,6,9]-4-28
[0,1,2,4]-4-2	[0,2,4,7]-4-22	
[0,1,3,4]-4-3	[0,2,5,7]-4-23	
[0,1,2,5]-4-4	[0,2,4,8]-4-24	
[0,1,2,6]-4-5	[0,2,6,8]-4-25	
[0,1,2,7]-4-6	[0,3,5,8]-4-26	
[0,1,4,5]-4-7	[0,2,5,8]-4-27	
[0,1,5,6]-4-8		
[0,1,6,7]-4-9		
[0,2,3,5]-4-10		
[0,1,3,5]-4-11		
[0,2,3,6]-4-12		
[0,1,3,6]-4-13		
[0,2,3,7]-4-14		
[0,1,4,6]-4-Z15		
[0,1,5,7]-4-16		
[0,3,4,7]-4-17		
[0,1,4,7]-4-18		
[0,1,4,8]-4-19		
[0,1,5,8]-4-20		
[0,1,3,7]-4-Z29		

This family classification has the advantage of ease for both visual and aural use. The great imbalance in membership does limit the value of the classification—there are twenty-one tetrachords in family 1, seven in family 2, and one in family 3—but it can be used with some benefit in the early stages of work on tetrachords.

EXERCISE 5.1: Interval-content exercise

Four-note fragments should be played, either as melodies or as simultaneities, with progressively greater registral dispersal. Identify the interval content families. If a tetrachord is in family 1 sing the two pitches making up i(1); if the tetrachord is in family 2 sing the two pitches making up i(2).

In dealing with tetrachords it is also useful to work with the concept of a three-note subset type. In the tetrachord type [0,1,2,3]-4-1 we can describe the trichord content by eliminating each of the elements of the tetrachord, thereby producing four trichordal subsets. To use the example of [0,1,2,3]-4-1, made up of the pitch classes {0,1,2,3}: eliminating {0} leaves {1,2,3}, which gives the trichord type [0,1,2]-3-1; eliminating {1} leaves {0,2,3}, which gives the trichord type [0,1,3]-3-2; eliminating {2} leaves {0,1,3}, which gives the trichord type [0,1,3]-3-2; and eliminating {3} leaves {0,1,2}, which gives the trichord type [0,1,2]-3-1 (see ill. 5.2). In summary, the tetrachord type [0,1,2,3]-4-1 includes two instances of 3-1-[0,1,2] and two of 3-2-[0,1,3].

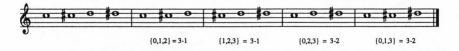

{0,1,2} = 3-1   {1,2,3} = 3-1   {0,2,3} = 3-2   {0,1,3} = 3-2

5.2. Trichordal subset content for [0,1,2,3]-4-1

DEFINITION 5.1: *Z-related set classes* Two set classes that have the same interval content, as shown in their interval vector, but not the same normal order name are said to be a Z-related pair. The members of a Z-related pair differ in their trichordal subset content and superset membership characteristics, and are related neither by transposition nor by inversion.

Two of the twenty-nine tetrachords, 4-Z15-[0,1,4,6] and 4-Z29-[0,1,3,7], have the same interval content, as shown in their interval vector <1,1,1, 1,1,1>. But they do not have the same normal order name, and therefore cannot be mapped onto each other by transposition or inversion. Since interval content has so far been the primary cue to the ear for identifying and characterizing tetrachords, we must find another basis for differentiating between the members of these "Z-related" pairs, which become much more numerous among sets of five and six members. One cue is trichordal subset content. In the case of 4-Z15-[0,1,4,6] these subset types are 3-3-[0,1,4], 3-5-[0,1,6], 3-8-[0,2,6], and 3-7-[0,2,5] (see ill. 5.3a). For 4-Z29-[0,1,3,7] the

{5,6,9,11} = [0,1,4,6]-4-Z15   {5,6,9} = [0,1,4]-3-3   {5,6,11} = [0,1,6]-3-5   {5,9,11} = [0,2,6]-3-8   {6,9,11} = [0,2,5]-3-7

5.3a. Subsets for 4-Z15-[0,1,4,6]

subset types are 3-2-[0,1,3], 3-5-[0,1,6], 3-8-[0,2,6], and 3-11-[0,3,7] (see ill. 5.3b).

{9,10,0,4} = [0,1,3,7]-4-Z29   {9,10,0} = [0,1,3]-3-2   {9,10,4} = [0,1,6]-3-5   {10,0,4} = [0,2,6]-3-8   {9,0,4} = [0,3,7]-3-11

5.3b. Subsets for 4-Z29-[0,1,3,7]

In this Z-related pair, we regard 3-3 as a distinctive aural feature for 4-Z15, and 3-11 as one for 4-Z29. Another cue is superset relations: 4-Z29-[0,1,3,7] is a diatonic subset; 4-Z15-[0,1,4,6] is not.

EXERCISE 5.2: Distinguishing Z-related set classes

The pianist plays a four-note melody or four-note chord representing either set class 4-Z15-[0,1,4,6] or set class 4-Z29-[0,1,3,7]. Using the cues of superset and subset characteristics, figure out which set class is being played.

The true identity of a tetrachordal set class can be defined as its total subset content: *dyadic,* as expressed in the six-digit *interval vector,* and *trichordal,* as expressed in its trichordal subset makeup. Subset content is both a more logical and a more aurally vivid badge of identification for the tetrachordal set class than is normal order.

Another system of classification, also an extension of the one proposed with regard to trichords, deals with membership in the two transpositions of the whole-tone hexachord: {0,2,4,6,8,10} and {1,3,5,7,9,11}. In whole-tone group 1, all four members of the tetrachord are part of one of the whole-tone hexachords. In whole-tone group 2, three of the four members of the tetrachord are in one of the whole-tone hexachords and one is in the other. (In other words, there is one instance of one of the "whole-tone trichord types," 3-6-[0,2,4], 3-8-[0,2,6], and 3-12-[0,4,8].) In whole-tone group 3, two of the four members of the hexachords are in one whole-tone hexachord and two are in the

5.4a. Whole-tone group 4-16

5.4b. Whole-tone group 4-14

other. Membership in whole-tone collections can be ascertained by the odd and even numbers in the normal order name. For example, in 4-16-[0,1,5,7] (see ill. 5.4a), three tones represented by the odd-numbered symbols [1,5,7] belong to one whole-tone collection, and one tone represented by the even-numbered symbol [0] belongs to the other. Therefore 4-16 belongs to whole-tone group 2. In 4-14-[0,2,3,7] (see ill. 5.4b), two tones represented by the even-numbered symbols [0,2] belong to one whole-tone collection and form i(2), and the other

TABLE 5.2. Tetrachordal set classes in whole-tone groups

Group 1 (4 + 0)	Group 2 (3 + 1)	Group 3 (2 + 2)
[0,2,4,6]-4-21	[0,1,2,4]-4-2	[0,1,2,3]-4-1
[0,2,4,8]-4-24	[0,1,2,6]-4-5	[0,1,3,4]-4-3
[0,2,6,8]-4-25	[0,1,3,5]-4-11	[0,1,2,5]-4-4
	[0,2,3,6]-4-12	[0,1,2,7]-4-6
	[0,1,4,6]-4-Z15	[0,1,4,5]-4-7
	[0,1,5,7]-4-16	[0,1,5,6]-4-8
	[0,1,4,8]-4-19	[0,1,6,7]-4-9
	[0,2,4,7]-4-22	[0,2,3,5]-4-10
	[0,2,5,8]-4-27	[0,1,3,6]-4-13
	[0,1,3,7]-4-Z29	[0,2,3,7]-4-14
		[0,3,4,7]-4-17
		[0,1,4,7]-4-18
		[0,1,5,8]-4-20
		[0,2,5,7]-4-23
		[0,3,5,8]-4-26
		[0,3,6,9]-4-28

two, represented by the odd-numbered symbols [3,7], belong to the other and form i(4). Therefore 4-14 belongs to whole-tone group 3.

Tetrachords belonging to whole-tone group 1 can be called "whole-tone tetrachords," for they evoke the sound of a complete whole-tone hexachord. The groups shown in table 5.2 result from the above method of classification.

The distribution is more even in this whole-tone method of classification than in the family method based on interval content: there are three tetrachord types in group 1, ten in group 2, and sixteen in group 3. The ability to hear whole-tone adherences of tetrachords can be enhanced by doing the following exercise:

EXERCISE 5.3: Whole-tone exercises

  a) **A four-note simultaneity or melodic succession within an octave is played. In response, sing the whole-tone scale that contains four, three, or two of the pitches of the chord or melodic succession and accent those pitches; then sing the whole-tone scale that contains the remaining one or two pitches of the chord or melodic succession and accent those pitches.**
  b) **For a more difficult version of this exercise, sing only those pitches of each whole-tone scale that appear in the chord or melodic succession.**

To group tetrachordal set class types in supersets appeals directly to most ears. The supersets I have chosen for this purpose are useful to know for any number of reasons: (1) the *diatonic superset* [0,1,3,5,6,8,10]-7-35; (2) the *octatonic superset* [0,1,3,4,6,7,9,10]-8-28; and (3) the *whole-tone superset* [0,2,4,6,8,10]-6-35. These categories account for all but seven of the twenty-nine tetrachords. Five of these seven are *supersets of the chromatic trichord* [0,1,2]-3-1, and one is a superset of the augmented trichord [0,4,8]-3-12. Only one tetrachordal set class, [0,1,4,5]-4-7, is in none of these superset or subset groups.

The following is a list of supersets and subsets in the categories given above. *If a tetrachord type occurs more than once in a given superset, the number of times it appears is in parentheses after the set class number:*

1. *Tetrachordal members of the diatonic collection* (pentatonic subsets in boldface)

   [0,1,5,6]-4-8
   [0,2,3,5]-4-10 (2)
   [0,1,3,5]-4-11 (4)
   [0,1,3,6]-4-13 (2)
   [0,2,3,7]-4-14 (4)
   [0,1,5,7]-4-16 (2)
   [0,1,5,8]-4-20 (2)
   [0,2,4,6]-4-21
   [0,2,4,7]-4-22 (6)
   [0,2,5,7]-4-23 (4)
   [0,3,5,8]-4-26 (3)
   [0,2,5,8]-4-27 (2)
   [0,1,3,7]-4-Z29 (2)

2. *Tetrachordal members of the octatonic collection.* Note that membership in the octatonic collection depends on the presence of *two* unordered pitch class intervals of type 3, type 6, or both. The set class 4-18-[0,1,4,7] contains one instance of i(3), [1,4], and one instance of i(6), [1,7], and is therefore a subset of the octatonic collection.

   [0,1,3,4]-4-3 (4)
   [0,1,6,7]-4-9 (2)
   [0,2,3,5]-4-10 (4)
   [0,2,3,6]-4-12 (8)
   [0,1,3,6]-4-13 (8)
   [0,1,4,6]-4-Z15 (8)
   [0,3,4,7]-4-17 (4)
   [0,1,4,7]-4-18 (8)
   [0,2,6,8]-4-25 (2)
   [0,3,5,8]-4-26 (4)
   [0,2,5,8]-4-27 (8)
   [0,3,6,9]-4-28 (2)
   [0,1,3,7]-4-Z29 (8)

3. *Tetrachordal members of the whole-tone collection* (see also whole-tone group 1 in table 5.2)

   [0,2,4,6]-4-21 (6)
   [0,2,4,8]-4-24 (6)
   [0,2,6,8]-4-25 (3)

4. *Tetrachordal supersets of the chromatic trichord*

   4-1-[0,1,2,3] contains 3-1 twice
   4-2-[0,1,2,4]
   4-4-[0,1,2,5]
   4-5-[0,1,2,6]
   4-6-[0,1,2,7]

5. *Tetrachordal supersets of the augmented trichord*

   4-19-[0,1,4,8]
   4-24-[0,2,4,8]

EXERCISE 5.4: Superset exercise (for one)

Play a four-note broken chord within the ambitus of an octave, then sing a compact form of the diatonic, octatonic, or whole-tone superset *that includes it,* or the chromatic or augmented trichord *that it includes*. When singing the superset, emphasize the pitches of the original four-note chord. For example, play slowly $<-10,-6,-5,-1>$, a form of [0,1,5,8]-4-20. Then sing $<-10,-8,-6,-5,-3,-1,+1,+2> = <2,4,6,7,9,11,1,2>$ (the D major scale), emphasizing the first, third, fourth, and sixth pitches (which make up the form of 4-20 just heard).

Learning the tetrachords by means of their membership in these three superset groups accomplishes two things: it is an intuitively workable approach to identifying the tetrachords, and it enforces a more acute hearing of the characteristics of the supersets. Identifying the supersets in this way leads naturally to the modal approach (see chapter 6) and relates strongly to the way Debussy, Bartók, Stravinsky, and many other twentieth-century composers used modes independently of characteristics of dissonance and consonance.

Another way to categorize tetrachords grows out of a skill developed in chapter 4: they can be categorized according to whether they include the inversionally symmetrical trichords [0,1,2]-3-1, [0,2,4]-3-6, [0,2,7]-3-9, [0,3,6]-3-10, and [0,4,8]-3-12.

The trichords in table 5.3 are contained in the tetrachords listed below them.

TABLE 5.3. Symmetrical trichord set class
types as contained in tetrachordal set classes

3-1	3-6	3-9	3-10	3-12	None
4-1	4-2	4-6	4-12	4-19	4-3
4-2	4-11	4-14	4-13	4-24	4-7
4-4	4-21	4-16	4-18		4-8
4-5	4-22	4-22	4-27		4-9
4-6	4-24	4-23	4-28		4-10
					4-Z15
					4-17
					4-20
					4-25
					4-26
					4-Z29

EXERCISE 5.5: Inclusion of inversionally symmetrical trichord
types: Singing exercise

**A four-note melodic figure or chord within the ambitus of an octave is played; specify
which of the symmetrical *trichord* types is present (if any), and then sing the pitches that
constitute that trichord type.**

The following are some common tetrachords that are easy to identify by eye or
ear:

[0,1,2,3]-4-1, "chromatic," a tetrachord that could be presented as four consecutive
members of a chromatic scale;

[0,2,4,6]-4-21, "whole-tone," a tetrachord that could be presented as four consecutive members of a whole-tone scale;

[0,3,6,9]-4-28, "diminished," a tetrachord that could be presented as four consecutive i<3> representatives of the diminished seventh chord;

[0,2,5,7]-4-23, "fourth-chord," a tetrachord that could be presented as four consecutive members of the circle of fifths;

[0,2,5,8]-4-27, familiar from tonal contexts as the dominant seventh chord (*inversionally* equivalent to the half-diminished seventh chord);

[0,3,5,8]-4-26, familiar from tonal contexts as the minor seventh chord;

[0,1,3,4]-4-3, "octatonic tetrachord 1," a tetrachord that could be presented as four
consecutive members of an octatonic scale starting with a half-step;

[0,2,3,5]-4-10, "octatonic tetrachord 2," a tetrachord that could be presented as four
consecutive members of an octatonic scale starting with a whole-step;

[0,1,3,5]-4-11, "major tetrachord 1," a tetrachord that could be presented as the first
four degrees of a major scale (inversionally equivalent to "Phrygian 1");

[0,1,5,8]-4-20, familiar from tonal contexts as the major seventh chord (this tetrachord is inversionally symmetrical, although this is not evident from the normal order name).

EXERCISE 5.6: Set class identification

a) **To practice aural identification of the preceding set classes, divide the ten set classes into the three groups indicated below. The pianist plays chords selected from each group in a variety of spacings; identify each set class.**

   [0,1,2,3]-4-1
   [0,1,3,5]-4-11
   [0,1,5,8]-4-20
   [0,3,5,8]-4-26

   [0,2,3,5]-4-10
   [0,2,4,6]-4-21
   [0,2,5,7]-4-23

   [0,1,3,4]-4-3
   [0,2,5,8]-4-27
   [0,3,6,9]-4-28

b) **Perform the same exercise using the two following larger groups:**

   [0,1,2,3]-4-1
   [0,1,3,4]-4-3
   [0,1,3,5]-4-11
   [0,2,5,7]-4-23
   [0,2,5,8]-4-27

   [0,2,3,5]-4-10
   [0,1,5,8]-4-20
   [0,2,4,6]-4-21
   [0,3,5,8]-4-26
   [0,3,6,9]-4-28

c) **Perform the same exercise using all ten set classes cited above.**

A musically significant way to conceptualize the relation of the dyad with the interval of transposition in most symmetrical tetrachords is by *multiplying* one i(n) type by the other.

DEFINITION 5.2: *Multiplication*   When two instances of the same interval i(p) occur, separated by interval i(q), the resulting set can be called i(p) multiplied by i(q). We can thus generate symmetrical tetrachords through the multiplication of two dyads (examples follow as part of exercise 5.7).

Bartók's melodies, characterized by a predominance of symmetrical set classes of all sizes, demonstrate clearly the concept of multiplication. In ill. 5.5, from Bartók's *Mikrokosmos*, the spatial characteristics of the melody demonstrate the multiplication of interval type 2 at transposition level 5, producing 4-23-[0,2,5,7]. In this example one can also understand the two dyads in a relation of inversion.[1]

5.5. Bartók: *Mikrokosmos*, vol. 1, no. 36: i(2) and its T^P_{-5} = i(2) × i(5) = {0,2,7,9} = {7,9,0,2} = 4-23-[0,2,5,7]

EXERCISE 5.7: Tetrachord melodies: Dictation and sight-singing

One or two melodies for each tetrachordal set class follow each entry on the list of tetrachords. These melodies are to be used for dictation and for sight-singing. In doing dictation, the melody should be heard until it is memorized, then written down; after this, the newly written dictation can be compared with the melody. To focus attention on the pitch relations, dictations should be done initially with a simplified rhythm of one pitch to each beat. At a more advanced stage, rhythmic values can be incorporated into the dictation. In sight-singing, use pitch class numbers. As in the comparable section in chapter 4, practice all the transpositions and inversions: the pitch class numbers as well as the tones sung should reflect the transformation. In all sight-singing and practicing of transpositions and inversions, follow the stages suggested in exercise 2.6. Practice the transpositions and inversions instrumentally as well as vocally.

Melodies illustrating multiplication are included among the tetrachord melodies that follow. Like the other tetrachord melodies these should be used for both dictation and sight-singing, and listeners should attempt to identify the multiplication relation being illustrated. The melodies should also be sung in inversion at the levels that maintain pitch class invariance.

The complete list of set classes and their attributes identifies the key characteristics of each tetrachordal set class. It also summarizes much of the information contained in the tables of this chapter, but emphasizes the individual set class rather than the properties that were the subject of earlier exercises and discussion.

LIST OF TETRACHORDS

4-1
[0,1,2,3]
Inversionally symmetrical
Interval vector <3,2,1,0,0,0>
Trichord subset content: 3-1(2), 3-2(2)
Twelve different pitch class collections
Family 1, contains i(1)
Whole-tone group 3 (2 + 2)
Chromatic trichord superset

This is the "chromatic" tetrachord, which maximizes i(1) and contains two distinct instances of the chromatic trichord, 3-1. It is not characteristic of any common modes. Although we intuitively tend to imagine it as a cluster, it can of course be dispersed like any other set class over a broad pitch space.

Multiplicative melody for 4-1-[0,1,2,3]: i(2) and its T_{+1}^P = i(1) and its T_{+2}^P = i(1) × i(2) = {0,1,2,3}; also sing at I_3

4-2
[0,1,2,4]
Interval vector <2,2,1,1,0,0>
Trichord subset content: 3-1, 3-2, 3-3, 3-6
Family 1, contains i(1)
Whole-tone group 2 (3 + 1)
Chromatic trichord superset

This tetrachord contains two of the inversionally symmetrical trichords: the chromatic trichord 3-1, and the whole-tone trichord 3-6.

Melody for 4-2-[0,1,2,4]. {1,2,3,5}

Melody for 4-2-[0,1,2,4]. {2,4,5,6} = {6,5,4,2}

4-3

[0,1,3,4]

Inversionally symmetrical

Twelve different pitch class collections

Interval vector $<2,1,2,1,0,0>$

Trichord subset content: 3-2(2), 3-3(2)

Family 1, contains i(1)

Whole-tone group 3 (2 + 2)

Octatonic subset, but not diatonic subset

One expression of this tetrachord is as a series of four consecutive tones of the octatonic scale. It contains two occurrences each of [0,1,3]-3-2 and [0,1,4]-3-3.

Multiplicative melody for 4-3-[0,1,3,4]: i(3) and its T_{-1}^P = i(1) and its T_3 = i(1) × i(3) = {3,4,6,7}; also sing at I_{10}

4-4

[0,1,2,5]

Interval vector $< 2,1,1,1,1,0>$

Trichord subset content: 3-1, 3-3, 3-4, 3-7

Family 1, contains i(1)

Whole-tone group 3 (2 + 2)

Chromatic trichord superset

Melody for 4-4-[0,1,2,5]. {4,5,6,9}

Melody for 4-4-[0,1,2,5]. {5,8,9,10} = {10,9,8,5}

4-5
[0,1,2,6]
Interval vector <2,1,0,1,1,1>
Trichord subset content: 3-1, 3-4, 3-5, 3-8
Family 1, contains i(1)
Whole-tone group 2 (3 + 1)
Chromatic trichord superset

Melody for 4-5-[0,1,2,6]. {0,6,7,8} = {6,7,8,0}

Melody for 4-5-[0,1,2,6]. {0,1,7,11} = {1,0,11,7}

4-6
[0,1,2,7]
Inversionally symmetrical
Twelve different pitch class collections
Interval vector <2,1,0,0,2,1>
Trichord subset content: 3-1, 3-5(2), 3-9
Family 1, contains i(1)
Whole-tone group 3 (2 + 2)
Chromatic trichord superset

This tetrachord contains two inversionally symmetrical trichord types, the "chromatic" trichord 3-1 and the "fourth-chord" 3-9, as well as two instances of [0,1,6]-3-5.

Melody for 4-6-[0,1,2,7]. {3,8,9,10} = {8,9,10,3}

4-7

[0,1,4,5]

Inversionally symmetrical

Twelve different pitch class collections

Interval vector <2,0,1,2,1,0>

Trichord subset content: 3-3(2), 3-4(2)

Family 1, contains i(1)

Whole-tone group 3 (2 + 2)

   This tetrachord is conveniently identifiable in one tonal manifestation, as the upper tetrachord of the "harmonic minor" scale. It contains two instances each of [0,1,4]-3-3 and [0,1,5]-3-4.

Multiplicative melody for 4-7-[0,1,4,5]: i(4) and its T^P_{-1} = i(1) and its T^P_{-8} = i(1) × i(4) = {9,10,1,2}; also sing at I_{11}

4-8

[0,1,5,6]

Inversionally symmetrical

Twelve different pitch class collections

Interval vector <2,0,0,1,2,1>

Trichord subset content: 3-4(2), 3-5(2)

Family 1, contains i(1)

Whole-tone group 3 (2 + 2)

Diatonic subset

   A helpful tonal handle on this tetrachord is that it not only is a diatonic subset but also contains the two "half-steps" of the diatonic collection. It contains two occurrences each of [0,1,5]-3-4 and [0,1,6]-3-5.

Multiplicative melody for 4-8-[0,1,5,6]: i(1) and its T^P_{+5} = i(5) and its T^P_{-1} = i(1) × i(5) = {3,4,8,9}; also sing at I_0

4-9

[0,1,6,7]

Inversionally symmetrical

Transpositionally symmetrical

Six different pitch class collections

Interval vector <2,0,0,0,2,2>

Trichord subset content: 3-5(4)

Family 1, contains i(1)

Whole-tone group 3 (2 + 2)

Octatonic subset, but not diatonic subset

Besides being a typically octatonic subset, this tetrachord appears widely in the music of composers as diverse as Bartók and Webern. Its only trichordal subset type is [0,1,6]-3-5.

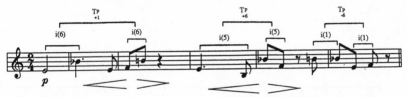

Multiplicative melody for 4-9-[0,1,6,7]: i(6) and its T_{+1}^P = i(5) and its T_{+6}^P = i(1) and its T_5 = i(1) × i(6) or i(5) × i(6) = {4,5,10,11}; also sing at I_9, I_3, and T_6 (transposition up or down six semitones)

4-10

[0,2,3,5]

Inversionally symmetrical

Twelve different pitch class collections

Interval vector <1,2,2,0,1,0>

Trichord subset content: 3-2(2), 3-7(2)

Family 1, contains i(1)

Whole-tone group 3 (2 + 2)

Diatonic subset

This tetrachord appears in its most compact pitch manifestation as the initial tetrachord of the minor and Dorian modes. It contains two occurrences each of [0,1,3]-3-2 and [0,2,5]-3-7.

Multiplicative melody for 4-10-[0,2,3,5]: i(3) and its T_{+2}^P = i(2) and its T_{+3}^P = i(2) × i(3) = {5,7,8,10}; also sing at I_3

4-11
[0,1,3,5]
Interval vector <1,2,1,1,1,0>
Trichord subset content: 3-2, 3-4, 3-6, 3-7
Family 1, contains i(1)
Whole-tone group 2 (3 + 1)
Diatonic subset

The initial tetrachords of the Phrygian mode and the major scale are examples of this set class type. It contains one inversionally symmetrical trichord type, [0,2,4]-3-6.

Melody for 4-11-[0,1,3,5]. {1,2,4,6}

Melody for 4-11-[0,1,3,5]. {2,4,6,7} = {7,6,4,2}

4-12
[0,2,3,6]
Interval vector <1,1,2,1,0,1>
Trichord subset content: 3-2, 3-3, 3-8, 3-10
Family 1, contains i(1)
Whole-tone group 2 (3 + 1)
Octatonic subset, but not diatonic subset

One form of this subset is as an octatonic mode segment with one "step" missing: {0,2,3,_,6}. It contains one instance of the "diminished trichord" [0,3,6]-3-10.

Melody for 4-12-[0,2,3,6]. {3,5,6,9}

Melody for 4-12-[0,2,3,6]. {4,7,8,10} = {10,8,7,4}

4-13
[0,1,3,6]
Interval vector <1,1,2,0,1,1>
Trichord subset content: 3-2, 3-5, 3-7, 3-10
Family 1, contains i(1)
Whole-tone group 3 (2 + 2)
Diatonic subset
    The comments pertaining to 4-12 are equally appropriate to this set.

Melody for 4-13-[0,1,3,6]. {5,6,8,11}

Melody for 4-13-[0,1,3,6]. {5,8,10,11} = {11,10,8,5}

4-14
[0,2,3,7]
Interval vector <1,1,1,1,2,0>
Trichord subset content: 3-2, 3-4, 3-9, 3-11
Family 1, contains i(1)
Whole-tone group 3 (2 + 2)
Diatonic subset
    This set could appear as the first five steps of the minor mode, with either
the fourth step missing (as in {0,2,3,_,7}) or the second step missing (as in
{0,_,4,5,7}). It contains one inversionally symmetrical trichord, the "fourth-
chord" [0,2,7]-3-9.

Melody for 4-14-[0,2,3,7]. {1,6,8,9} = {6,8,9,1}

Melody for 4-14-[0,2,3,7]. {0,2,7,11} = {2,0,11,7}

4-Z15
[0,1,4,6]
Interval vector <1,1,1,1,1,1>
Trichord subset content: 3-3, 3-5, 3-7, 3-8
Family 1, contains i(1)
Whole-tone group 2 (3 + 1)
Octatonic subset, but not diatonic subset

This is one of the two examples of an "all-interval tetrachord" (the other being 4-Z29), containing one example of each unordered interval type. It could appear as a contiguous segment of the octatonic mode with the third step missing: {0,1,_,4,6}.

Melody for 4-Z15-[0,1,4,6]. {0,2,8,9} = {8,9,0,2}

Melody for 4-Z15-[0,1,4,6]. {2,3,9,11} = {3,2,11,9}

4-16
[0,1,5,7]
Interval vector <1,1,0,1,2,1>
Trichord subset content: 3-4, 3-5, 3-8, 3-9
Family 1, contains i(1)
Whole-tone group 2 (3 + 1)
Diatonic subset

This could appear as the initial five notes of the Phrygian mode with the third degree missing, {0,1,_,5,7}, or as the initial five notes of the Mixolydian mode with the third degree missing, {0,2,_,6,7}. It contains the "fourth-chord," [0,2,7]-3-9.

Melody for 4-16-[0,1,5,7]. {3,5,10,11} = {10,11,3,5}

Melody for 4-16-[0,1,5,7]. {1,5,6,11} = {6,5,1,11}

4-17
[0,3,4,7]
Inversionally symmetrical
Twelve different pitch class collections
Interval vector <1,0,2,2,1,0>
Trichord subset content: 3-3(2), 3-11(2)
Family 1, contains i(1)
Whole-tone group 3 (2 + 2)
Octatonic subset, but not diatonic subset

One polymodal use for this tetrachord is as the major-minor tetrachord (as in Bartók): a triad with both major and minor thirds. This set class contains two instances each of [0,1,4]-3-3 and [0,3,7]-3-11 (one each of the major and minor triads).

Multiplicative melody for 4-17-[0,3,4,7]: i(4) and its T_{-3}^P = i(3) and its T_{+8}^P = i(3) × i(4) = {2,5,6,9}; also sing at I_{11}

4-18
[0,1,4,7]
Interval vector <1,0,2,1,1,1>
Trichord subset content: 3-3, 3-5, 3-10, 3-11
Family 1, contains i(1)
Whole-tone group 3 (2 + 2)
Octatonic subset, but not diatonic subset

This tetrachord contains both the major (or minor) triad and one inversionally symmetrical trichord: the "diminished" trichord, [0,3,6]-3-10. It is a favorite of Schoenberg.

Melody for 4-18-[0,1,4,7]. {0,1,4,7}

Melody for 4-18-[0,1,4,7]. {1,4,7,8} = {8,7,4,1}

4-19
[0,1,4,8]
Interval vector <1,0,1,3,1,0>
Trichord subset content: 3-3, 3-4, 3-11, 3-12
Family 1, contains i(1)
Whole-tone group 2 (3 + 1)
Augmented trichord superset

This tetrachord, another favorite of Schoenberg, is one of two tetrachords that contain the "augmented" trichord 3-12-[0,4,8], one of the most conspicuous of the inversionally symmetrical trichords. It also contains the major (or minor) trichord [0,3,7]-3-11.

Melody for 4-19-[0,1,4,8]. {3,4,7,11}

Melody for 4-19-[0,1,4,8]. {0,4,7,8} = {8,7,4,0}

4-20
[0,1,5,8]
Inversionally symmetrical
Twelve different pitch class collections
Interval vector <1,0,1,2,2,0>
Trichord subset content: 3-4(2), 3-11(2)
Family 1, contains i(1)
Whole-tone group 3 (2 + 2)
Diatonic subset

This is one of only four tetrachords to contain two instances of [0,3,7]. It can appear as a major seventh chord.

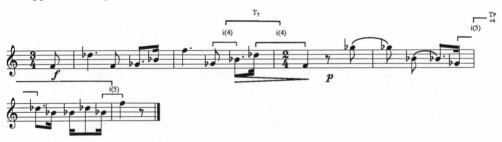

Multiplicative melody for 4-20-[0,1,5,8]: i(4) and its T_7 = i(5) and its T_{+4}^P = i(4) × i(5) = {1,5,6,10} = {5,6,10,1}; also sing at I_{11}

4-21
[0,2,4,6]
Inversionally symmetrical
Twelve different pitch class collections
Interval vector <0,3,0,2,0,1>
Trichord subset content: 3-6(2), 3-8(2)
Family 2, contains i(2) but not i(1)
Whole-tone group 1 (4 + 0)
Diatonic subset

This set could appear as a contiguous segment of the whole-tone mode. It contains two instances each of [0,2,4]-3-6 and [0,2,6]-3-8.

Multiplicative melody for 4-21-[0,2,4,6]: i(4) and its T_{+2}^P = i(2) and its T_{+4}^P = i(2) × i(4) = {0,2,8,10} = {8,10,0,2}; also sing at I_{10}

4-22
[0,2,4,7]
Interval vector <0,2,1,1,2,0>
Trichord subset content: 3-6, 3-7, 3-9, 3-11
Family 2, contains i(2) but not i(1)
Whole-tone group 2 (3 + 1)
Diatonic subset, one of the three tetrachordal pentatonic subsets

This set could appear as the initial five notes of the major mode with the fourth degree missing, {0,2,4,_,7}, or as the initial five notes of the minor mode with the second degree missing, {0,_,3,5,7}. It contains two inversionally symmetrical trichords, 3-6-[0,2,4] and 3-9-[0,2,7].

Melody for 4-22-[0,2,4,7]. {2,7,9,11} = {7,9,11,2}

Melody for 4-22-[0,2,4,7]. {1,3,8,11} = {3,1,11,8}

4-23
[0,2,5,7]
Inversionally symmetrical
Twelve different pitch class collections
Interval vector <0,2,1,0,3,0>
Trichord subset content: 3-7(2), 3-9(2)
Family 2, contains i(2) but not i(1)
Whole-tone group 3 (2 + 2)
Diatonic subset, one of the three tetrachordal pentatonic subsets

This tetrachord has two instances each of [0,2,5]-3-7 and [0,2,7]-3-9. It could appear as the initial five notes of either the major or minor mode with the third degree missing: {0,2,_,5,7}.

Multiplicative melody for 4-23-[0,2,5,7]: i(2) and its T^P_{-7} = i(2) × i(5) = {2,4,9,11} = {9,11,2,4}; also sing at I_1

4-24
[0,2,4,8]
Inversionally symmetrical
Twelve different pitch class collections
Interval vector <0,2,0,3,0,1>
Trichord subset content: 3-6, 3-8(2), 3-12
Family 1, contains i(1)
Whole-tone group 1 (4 + 0)
Augmented trichord superset

This tetrachord, a whole-tone subset, contains the two inversionally symmetrical trichords [0,4,8]-3-12 and [0,2,4]-3-6, as well as two instances of [0,2,6]-3-8.

Melody for 4-24-[0,2,4,8]. {0,2,6,10} = {10,0,2,6}

4-25
[0,2,6,8]
Inversionally symmetrical
Transpositionally symmetrical
Six different pitch class collections
Interval vector <0,2,0,2,0,2>
Trichord subset content: 3-8(4)
Family 2, contains i(2) but not i(1)
Whole-tone group 1 (4 + 0)
Octatonic subset, but not diatonic subset

This whole-tone subset contains only one trichordal subset type: [0,2,6]-3-8.

Multiplicative melody for 4-25-[0,2,6,8]: i(2) and its T_{+6}^P = i(6) and its T_{+2}^P = i(4) and its T_6 = i(6) and its T_4 = i(4) × i(6) = {0,4,6,10} = {4,6,10,0}; also sing at I_{10}, I_4, and T_6 (transposition up or down six semitones)

4-26
[0,3,5,8]
Inversionally symmetrical
Twelve different pitch class collections
Interval vector <0,1,2,1,2,0>
Trichord subset content: 3-7(2), 3-11(2)
Family 2, contains i(2) but not i(1)
Whole-tone group 3 (2 + 2)
Diatonic subset, one of the three tetrachordal pentatonic subsets

One form of this tetrachord is the minor seventh chord. It contains two occurrences each of [0,2,5]-3-7 and [0,3,7]-3-11.

Multiplicative melody for 4-26-[0,3,5,8]: i(3) and its T_{+7}^P = i(5) and its T_{-3}^P = i(3) × i(5) = {2,4,7,11} = {11,2,4,7}; also sing at I_6

4-27
[0,2,5,8]
Interval vector <0,1,2,1,1,1>
Trichord subset content: 3-7, 3-8, 3-10, 3-11
Family 2, contains i(2) but not i(1)
Whole-tone group 2 (3 + 1)
Diatonic subset

This set can occur as the half-diminished seventh chord {0,3,6,10} or as the dominant seventh chord {0,4,7,10}. It contains one inversionally symmetrical trichord: [0,3,6]-3-10, the "diminished triad."

Melody for 4-27-[0,2,5,8]. {1,3,6,9}

Melody for 4-27-[0,2,5,8]. {2,5,8,10} = {10,8,5,2}

4-28
[0,3,6,9]
Inversionally symmetrical
Transpositionally symmetrical
Three different pitch class collections
Interval vector <0,0,4,0,0,2>
Trichord subset content: 3-10(4)
Family 3, neither i(1) nor i(2)
Whole-tone group 3 (2 + 2)
Octatonic subset, but not diatonic subset

This set, the "diminished seventh tetrachord," maximizes i(3) and contains only one trichordal subset, [0,3,6]-3-10. It occurs twice in the octatonic mode.

Multiplicative melody for 4-28-[0,3,6,9]. {0,3,6,9}; also sing at I_9, I_6, I_3, I_0, T_9, T_6, and T_3

4-Z29
[0,1,3,7]
Interval vector <1,1,1,1,1,1>
Trichord subset content: 3-2, 3-5, 3-8, 3-11
Family 1, contains i(1)
Whole-tone group 2 (3 + 1)
Diatonic subset

Like 4-Z15, this set class is an all-interval tetrachord and an octatonic subset. Unlike 4-Z15, this set contains 3-11 as a subset.

Melody for 4-Z29-[0,1,3,7]. {4,5,7,11}

Melody for 4-Z29-[0,1,3,7]. {0,5,9,11} = {0,11,9,5}

Although the greater number of tetrachordal set types causes difficulty, the exercises in chapter 4 for learning and manipulating trichords are also applicable to tetrachords and larger sets (this is especially true of the modal singing exercise and the arpeggio exercise), as are the processes relating trichord pairs.

EXERCISE 5.8: Comparing tetrachord pairs

An important exercise for achieving familiarity with tetrachords is the exercise measuring degrees of similarity between tetrachord pairs, used in chapter 4 for trichords (exercise 4.7). It is especially useful if students take turns performing the exercise at the keyboard: two representatives of a given tetrachordal set class type are played. Do they have the same rip<(n)>? Are they related by pitch class transposition or inversion?

In relating pairs of instances of tetrachord types by transpositions and inversion, we should be sensitive to three levels of invariance: dyadic invariance, as described in chapter 3, trichordal invariance, as described in chapter 4, and full tetrachordal invariance, as occasioned by the properties of transpositional and inversional symmetry in the twenty-nine tetrachords. Fifteen of the twenty-nine tetrachordal set class types are inversionally symmetrical, and three are transpositionally symmetrical: [0,1,6,7]-4-9, [0,2,6,8]-4-25, and [0,3,6,9]-4-28. The first two of these are characterized by two more *degrees of symmetry* than the other inversionally symmetrical tetrachords, and the third is characterized by three *additional* degrees of symmetry—it is most nearly analogous to the trichord [0,4,8]-3-12 and the dyad type i(6), with regard both to its degrees of symmetry and to its potential to divide the octave equally in pitch space.

EXERCISE 5.9: Invariance through singing

One of the inversionally or transpositionally symmetrical tetrachord types is played as a melodic fragment. Sing back a fragment that demonstrates dyadic invariance, one that demonstrates trichordal invariance, and one that demonstrates full tetrachordal invariance. In performing these operations, be aware that *pitch class invariance* is highlighted if it is also *pitch invariance*. But emphasizing the operation of transposition or inversion by making it *pitch transposition* or *pitch inversion* sometimes makes *pitch invariance* impossible (see ill. 5.6). In performing the exercise, decide whether *pitch invariance* or *pitch inversion* is the goal. The multiplicative melodies used in ex. 5.7 are well suited for this exercise.

In ill. 5.6a, the four-note phrase is transformed by pitch class inversion in such a way that *the pitches are invariant*. In this instance a stasis of pitch content is achieved, and the operation of inversion is not the obvious focus of what we hear. In ill. 5.6b the same four-note phrase is similarly transformed, but in this instance the focus of our hearing is the process of *pitch inversion*, because the register in which the pitch classes appear has been changed so that the contour inversion corresponds to the pitch class inversion.

5.6a. Inversion with pitch *invariance* emphasized

5.6b. Inversion with pitch *inversion* emphasized

For further work on inversional symmetry and invariance see appendix 2, groups 1–3.

EXERCISE 5.10: Tetrachord reading

As with trichords, the reading off of tetrachord types should be practiced with any one-voiced example, first by reading off adjacent tetrachords (the first four pitch classes of a melody, then the next four, and so on), then by overlapping tetrachord types (notes 1,2,3,4, then 2,3,4,5, then 3,4,5,6, and so on).

EXERCISE 5.11: Exercises with musical examples

The musical examples cited below should be played slowly by the pianist, until the analytic questions can be answered.

a) Listen to ex. 138: what is the rip series for each tetrachord within each measure? What are the tetrachordal set class types in each measure? If there are any recurrences of a set type, what is the relationship between their pc contents?

b) Listen to ex. 134: write the series of *pitch intervals* for each of the four four-note gestures in the first two measures. Now write the normal order name. What is the relation between pitch sets 1 and 3; between pitch sets 2 and 4? What transformation relates pc sets 1 and 2?

c) Listen to the first two bars of ex. 114: play and memorize the passage. Be able to play any pitch transposition of the tetrachord of each bar; be able to transpose the whole passage. Be able to play a pitch inversion of each tetrachord. Be able to play a pitch inversion of the whole passage.

d) Listen to ex. 114: listen for the four tetrachordal groups that make up this example; write the rip<( )> for each of them, then the set class types. If there are two or more of any type, try to describe the processes that relate them. If the sets are inversionally symmetrical types, try to describe the relationship as both pc transposition and pc inversion.

e) Listen to exx. 111 and 112: these seven-note phrase elements are best heard as a tetrachord plus a trichord. Try to hear the rip<( )> of each tetrachord and trichord, then the set class type. Describe as closely as possible the relations between the four pc tetrachords and the four pc trichords. Listen for contour and pitch as well as for pitch class relations.

f) Listen to ex. 110: identify the set class types of each four-note unit. Specify the relationship between any two members of the same type: pitch or pitch class transposition and inversion.

g) Listen to ex. 72: identify the three tetrachordal set class types into which the twelve-tone opening can be segmented (temporal order).

h) Listen to ex. 127: identify the tetrachord type formed by the soprano line of the first measure.

i) Listen to ex. 145: compare the two chords as forms of the same set class.

j) Listen to ex. 174 (to be played with the chords gently rolled): all the vertical four-note chords contain 3-3-[0,1,4], 3-4-[0,1,5], 3-5-[0,1,6], or 3-12-[0,4,8]. Using the abbreviation SATB (soprano, alto, tenor, bass) write which trichord types appear in the four-note chords, and in which voice combinations (for example, SAB, ATB).

k) Listen to ex. 174: write the rip<( )> and set class type of each chord. (Note that there are many repetitions.) Compare the rip<( )> of all chords of the same set class, and describe any systematic transformations you hear.

l) Listen to ex. 146: describe all the relationships you can hear between the rips of the two chords, as well as the pitch class transformations that relate them.

m) Listen to the first measure of ex. 156: first the alto flute, then the first two measures of the trumpet solo. What set classes are represented? What relationship do the pitch class collections have to each other? How many pitch classes do they have in common?

It is advisable to continue playing the musical examples slowly and repeat-edly, attempting a segmentation of the musical continuity based on set class, contour, and rhythm (as introduced in chapter 4). The repertoire of tetrachords introduced above provides an enlarged basis for these perceptions.

6
Sets of More Than Four Elements

Aural identification of pc sets of more than four elements is extremely problematic because of their sheer number (for example, there are thirty-seven five-note set classes, fifty six-note sets, and thirty-seven seven-note sets) and because of the subtlety of the differentiations between them in intervallic makeup. Particular difficulties accompany the proliferation of Z-related pairs of set classes, which have the same unordered pitch class interval (dyad) content, but have neither the same normal order name nor the same "Forte number." There is only one such pair of tetrachords, but there are three pairs of Z-related pentads (and septads), and fifteen pairs of Z-related hexachords, encompassing thirty of the fifty hexachordal set class types. The best way for the ear to distinguish between members of a Z-related pair is to compare their three- or four-note subsets and their superset content, which will always have some distinctive differences. But it takes additional, intensive study to *know* the distinctive properties of each member of each Z-related hexachord pair.

A characterization of larger sets through their subset and superset relations is the long but appropriate road to follow if precise identification of these sets by ear is the goal. Although a complete knowledge of all set types should be sought ultimately, two meaningful intermediary goals are to make general perceptions about most larger sets and to make specific identifications of a small selected number.

These goals will be worked on in three steps: (1) the identification of selected important and distinctive sets; (2) the grouping of sets by specific interval and by subset and superset characteristics; and where appropriate (3) the treatment of larger sets as modes with or without a gravitational center.

Prominent among sets that are important and relatively easy to recognize are the following supersets, most of which are introduced in chapters 4 and 5: the diatonic set 7-35 (and its prominent subset 6-32, the "do-re-mi-fa-sol-la" hexachord); the pentatonic set 5-35; the octatonic set 8-28 (and its only seven-note subset 7-31, with *its* complement 5-31); the whole-tone set 6-35 (and its only five-note subset 5-33, and *its* complement 7-33, the only superset of the whole-tone hexachord); the "magic hexachord" 6-20 (and its only five-note subset 5-21, and *its* complement 7-21, the only superset of the "magic" hexachord).

In the listing below the sets are characterized by their Forte number, their normal order name, their symmetrical properties, their interval vector, and their trichord subset content. Other incidental comments follow. An especially valuable tool for characterizing and identifying sets is the partitioning, where possible, of larger sets of six and eight members into inversionally or transpositionally related instances of subsets (for example, the copresence of two transpositionally related instances of a trichord type in a hexachord). Therefore possibilities are described both in words and in melodies that illustrate this property. Like the dyad melodies, trichord melodies, and tetrachord melodies, these illustrative melodies should be the basis of sight-singing and dictation exercises. When the melodies are played, listeners should be asked to identify the structures and processes that control the partitioning before they actually write down the melodies.

1. The diatonic set
    7-35
    [0,1,3,5,6,8,10]
    Inversionally symmetrical
    Twelve different pitch class collections
    Interval vector <2,5,4,3,6,1>
    Trichord subset content: 3-2(4), 3-4(4), 3-5(2), 3-6(3), 3-7(8), 3-8(2), 3-9(5), 3-10(1), 3-11(6)

The interval vector indicates a strict, "hierarchical" interval content: there are graded instances of the six unordered interval types (1–6). The "diatonic set" is expressed in the form of the major and natural minor scales, as well as the medieval modes. It has a rich subset content: there are nine different trichord types and seventeen different tetrachord types. Many will hear the set most readily as the "white-key" collection. The tetrachordal subset that occurs most often (six times) is 4-22-[0,2,4,7]; the trichordal subset that occurs most often in the diatonic collection is 3-7-[0,2,5] (eight times), but there are also six instances of the trichord type of the major (or minor) triad 3-11-[0,3,7].

6.1. 7-35-[0,1,3,5,6,8,10]. {0,2,4,5,7,9,11} = {11,0,2,4,5,7,9}. Stravinsky, *Petrouchka,* Danse russe

2. The "pentatonic" set
   5-35
   [0,2,4,7,9]
   Inversionally symmetrical
   Twelve different pitch class collections
   Interval vector <0,3,2,1,4,0>
   Trichord subset content: 3-6, 3-7(4), 3-9(3), 3-11(2)

This subset of the diatonic set occurs three times in it and is also its complement. As is typical of complement-related sets, the interval and subset contents of 7-35 and 5-35 are *proportionally* quite similar. In this set 3-7-[0,2,5] occurs four times and 3-9-[0,2,7] three times. This pentad is identifiable as the "black-key" collection and is characteristic of much Asian music. It is often the means by which "the Orient" is evoked in Western contexts, in music by composers as diverse as Debussy and Mahler. The absence of i(1) and i(6) makes this set eminently appropriate in a static, modal harmonic context, as in Debussy.

6.2. 5-35-[0,2,4,7,9]. {0,2,4,7,9}. Mahler, *Das Lied von der Erde*, opening theme

6.3. 5-35-[0,2,4,7,9]. {1,3,5,8,10}. Debussy, *Prélude à l'après-midi d'un faune*, m. 55

3. The "octatonic" set
8-28
[0,1,3,4,6,7,9,10]
Transpositionally and inversionally symmetrical
Three different pitch class collections
Interval vector <4,4,8,4,4,4>
Trichord subset content: 3-2(8), 3-3(8), 3-5(8), 3-7(8),'3-8(8), 3-10(8), 3-11(8)

This set is used characteristically in Bartók's and Stravinsky's music as a scale of alternating half- and whole-steps. One way to partition it is into two instances of the "diminished seventh" set 4-28-[0,3,6,9] (for example, {0,3,6,9} and its T_1). This partitioning can be interpreted in two ways: either as the transpositional multiplication of [0,3,6,9] by i(1), i(2), i(4), or i(5), or as the inversion of {0,3,6,9} in situations of sum 1, 4, 7, or 10. Another possible partitioning is into two instances of 4-3-[0,1,3,4], expressed multiplicatively as [0,1,3,4] × i(6). Yet another partitioning is into two instances of 4-9-[0,1,6,7]: [0,1,6,7] × i(3). The complement of this "octatonic set," 4-28, is the (third) diminished seventh chord.

The octatonic set has as many instances as possible of i(3) and i(6), and also of 3-10-[0,3,6], which occurs eight times. It also contains eight instances of the major (or minor) trichord 3-11-[0,3,7].

6.4. Multiplicative melody for 8-28-[0,1,3,4,6,7,9,10]: 4-9-[0,1,6,7] = {0,1,6,7} × i(3) = {3,4,9,10}; {0,1,3,4,6,7,9,10}

4. The "nearly octatonic" septad
   7-31
   [0,1,3,4,6,7,9]
   Interval vector <3,3,6,3,3,3>
   Trichord subset content: 3-2(5), 3-3(5), 3-5(5), 3-7(5), 3-8(5), 3-10(5), 3-11(5)

This is the only seven-element subset type of the octatonic set 8-28, and it contains the same subsets as 8-28. It maximizes i(6).

6.5. 7-31-[0,1,3,4,6,7,9]. {2,4,5,7,8,10,11} = {11,10,8,7,5,4,2}. Stravinsky, *Symphony of Psalms*, opening

5. The "diminished seventh plus one" pentad
   5-31
   [0,1,3,6,9]
   Interval vector <1,1,4,1,1,2>
   Trichord subset content: 3-2, 3-3, 3-5, 3-7, 3-8, 3-10(4), 3-11

This pentad is the complement of the "nearly octatonic" septad 7-31, and is the only five-note superset of the "diminished seventh" tetrachord 4-28.

6.6. Melody for 5-31-[0,1,3,6,9]. {0,3,6,9,11} = {0,11,9,6,3}

6. The "whole-tone" pentad
   5-33
   [0,2,4,6,8]
   Inversionally symmetrical
   Twelve different pitch class collections
   Interval vector <0,4,0,4,0,2>
   Trichord subset content: 3-6(3), 3-8(6), 3-12

This is the only five-element subset type that can be extracted from the whole-tone hexachord. It maximizes i(2), i(4), and i(6).

6.7. Melody for 5-33-[0,2,4,6,8]. {1,5,7,9,11} = {5,7,9,11,1}

7. The "almost whole-tone" septad
7-33
[0,1,2,4,6,8,10]
Inversionally symmetrical
Twelve different pitch class collections
Interval vector <2,6,2,6,2,3>
Trichord subset content: 3-1, 3-2(2), 3-3(2), 3-4(2), 3-5(2), 3-6(6), 3-7(2), 3-8(12), 3-9, 3-10, 3-11(2), 3-12(2)

As its Forte number indicates, 7-33 is the complement of 5-33. It can be viewed as 6-35—the whole-tone set—with any tone added (that is, it is the only seven-note superset of the whole-tone hexachord). Like 5-33 it maximizes i(2), i(4), and i(6), and 3-8-[0,2,6], but it contains all twelve trichordal set class types.

6.8. Melody for 7-33-[0,1,2,4,6,8,10]. {1,3,5,7,8,9,11} = {9,8,7,5,3,1,11}

8. 5-21
[0,1,4,5,8]
Interval vector <2,0,2,4,2,0>
Trichord subset content: 3-3(3), 3-4(3), 3-11(3), 3-12

The pentad 5-21 is the only five-note subset of 6-20, the magic hexachord (see below). Its interval vector reveals the same proportions of interval classes. It is the only pentad to contain three instances each of 3-3-[0,1,4] and 3-4-[0,1,5].

6.9. Melody for 5-21-[0,1,4,5,8]. {0,1,4,8,9} = {8,9,0,1,4}

9. 7-21
    [0,1,2,4,5,8,9]
    Interval vector <4,2,4,6,4,1>
    Trichord subset content: 3-1, 3-2(2), 3-3(7), 3-4(7), 3-5(2), 3-6, 3-7(2), 3-8(2),
        3-9, 3-10, 3-11(7), 3-12(2)

The set 7-21 is the complement of 5-21 and is the only seven-element superset of the magic hexachord 6-20 (see below). Its subset properties strongly resemble those of 5-21 and 6-20.

6.10. Melody for 7-21-[0,1,2,4,5,8,9]. {1,2,5,6,9,10,11} = {9,10,11,1,2,5,6}

10. Schoenberg's signature hexachord pair:
    a) 6-Z44
       [0,1,2,5,6,9]
       Interval vector <3,1,3,4,3,1>
       Trichord subset content: 3-1, 3-3(4), 3-4(4), 3-5(2), 3-7(2), 3-8, 3-10, 3-11(4),
           3-12
    b) 6-Z19
       [0,1,3,4,7,8]
       Interval vector <3,1,3,4,3,1>
       Trichord subset content: 3-2(2), 3-3(4), 3-4(4), 3-5(2), 3-8, 3-9, 3-10, 3-11(4),
           3-12

The hexachord 6-Z44 is Schoenberg's signature hexachord in a literal sense: one transposition of it contains the pitch classes Es (German for E-flat), C, H (German for B), B (German for B-flat), E, and G (Sch[ön]be[r]g). With its complement and Z-related hexachord 6-Z19, 6-Z44 plays a critical role in Schoenberg's music from before his twelve-tone period.

Both members of this Z-related pair contain four occurrences of [0,1,4]-3-3 and [0,3,7]-3-11, and both can demonstrate octatonic character (although neither is entirely a subset of the octatonic collection). 6-Z44 can be presented as [0,1,4] × i(5), 6-Z19 as [0,3,7] × i(1); 6-Z19 can demonstrate octatonic character (although neither is entirely a subset of the octatonic collection); and 6-Z44 contains the trichord [0,1,2]-3-1.

6.11a. 6-Z44-[0,1,2,5,6,9]. {2,3,4,7,10,11} = {4,3,2,11,10,7}. Schoenberg, Five Piano Pieces, op. 23, no. 4, opening

6.11b. Multiplicative melody for 6-Z19-[0,1,3,4,7,8]–3-11-[0,3,7] = {7,4,0} × i(1) = {8,5,1} = {0,1,4,5,7,8} = {8,7,5,4,1,0}

6.11c. Multiplicative melody for 6-Z44-[0,1,2,5,6,9]–3-3-[0,1,4] = {3,4,7} × i(5) = {8,9,0} = {0,3,4,7,8,9} = {9,8,7,4,3,0}

DEFINITION 6.1: *All-combinatoriality*   When the pitch classes of a hexa-chordal set class can be *both* transposed and inverted into their complement (the pitch classes that complete the twelve-pitch class collection), this property of the set class is called *all-combinatoriality*.

When only one transposition and one inversion of a hexachordal set class produce its complement, that set class is said to be of the *first-order combinatorial* type. When two transpositions and two inversions of a hexachordal set class produce its complement, that set class is said to be of the *second-order combinatorial* type.

None of the Z-related hexachords possesses the combinatorial property.

11. 6-1

[0,1,2,3,4,5]
"First-order" all-combinatorial: *one* transposition and *one* transposed inversion produce the complement
Inversionally symmetrical
Twelve different pitch class collections
Interval vector <5,4,3,2,1,0>
Trichord subset content: 3-1(4), 3-2(6), 3-3(4), 3-6(2), 3-7(2)

Like the diatonic septad 7-35, this "chromatic" hexachord is hierarchical in interval makeup, although the contents of the hierarchy are entirely different. Trichordal partitioning possibilities include $[0,1,2] \times i(3)$, $[0,2,4] \times i(1)$, $\{0,1,3\}$ and its I_5, and $\{0,1,4\}$ and its I_3. By partitioning it into trichords of the types 3-3 and 3-2, Webern frequently deployed this hexachord both in works predating his twelve-tone period and in works from it.

6.12. Multiplicative melody for 6-1-[0,1,2,3,4,5]. 3-6-[0,2,4] = $\{10,0,2\} \times i(1) = \{11,1,3\} = \{0,1,2,3,10,11\} = \{10,11,0,1,2,3\}$

12. 6-8

[0,2,3,4,5,7]
First order all-combinatorial
Inversionally symmetrical
Twelve different pitch class collections
Interval vector <3,4,3,2,3,0>
Trichord subset content: 3-1(2), 3-2(4), 3-3(2), 3-4(2), 3-6(2), 3-7(4), 3-9(2), 3-11(2)

This hexachord contains the chromatic tetrachord 4-1 and can be partitioned into two transpositionally related instances of the "whole-tone trichord" $[0,2,4] \times i(3)$; it can also be partitioned as $\{0,1,3\}$ and its I_{11}, $\{0,2,5\}$ and its I_3, and $\{0,1,5\}$ and its I_3.

6.13. Melody for 6-8-[0,2,3,4,5,7]. 3-7-[0,2,5] = $\{11,1,4\}$ and its I_1 = $\{2,0,9\}$ = $\{0,1,2,4,9,11\} = \{9,11,0,1,2,4\}$

13. 6-32

[0,2,4,5,7,9]

First order all-combinatorial

Inversionally symmetrical

Twelve different pitch class collections

Interval vector <1,4,3,2,5,0>

Trichord subset content: 3-2(2), 3-4(2), 3-6(2), 3-7(6), 3-9(4), 3-11(4)

This hexachord can be partitioned into two instances of the "whole-tone trichord," [0,2,4] × i(5) and {0,2,5} and its I_9. The interval vector reveals a "hierarchical" makeup, with different entries 0–5 for each unordered interval type. This is a quality that 6-32 has in common with 7-35, the "diatonic set" of which it is a subset. Moreover, one pitch representative of this set is the "major scale" hexachord "do-re-mi-fa-sol-la." The "pentatonic set" 5-35-[0,2,4,7,9] occurs twice in 6-32, which can be represented as a six-note segment of the circle of fifths and is thus most directly analogous in its "hierarchical" interval content to the chromatic hexachord 6-1.

6.14. Melody for 6-32-[0,2,4,5,7,9]. 3-7-[0,2,5] = {0,2,5} + its I_9 = {9,7,4} = {0,2,4,5,7,9}

14. 6-7

[0,1,2,6,7,8]

Second order all-combinatorial: *two* transpositions and *two* inversions produce its complement

Transpositionally and inversionally symmetrical

Six different pitch class collections

Interval vector <4,2,0,2,4,3>

Trichord subset content: 3-1(2), 3-4(4), 3-5(8), 3-8(4), 3-9(2)

This hexachord maximizes i(6). It can be partitioned into two instances of the chromatic trichord type, [0,1,2] × i(6) and [0,1,5] × i(6). It can also be partitioned into two inversionally related instances of the trichord type 3-5-[0,1,6]: {0,1,6} and its I_8.

6.15. Multiplicative melody for 6-7-[0,1,2,6,7,8]. 3-4-[0,1,5] = {1,2,6} × i(6) = {7,8,0} = {0,1,2,6,7,8}

15. 6-20

    [0,1,4,5,8,9]

    Third order all-combinatorial: *three* transpositions and *three* inversions produce
        the complement

    Transpositionally and inversionally symmetrical

    Four different pitch class collections

    Interval vector $<3,0,3,6,3,0>$

    Trichord subset content: 3-3(6), 3-4(6), 3-11(6), 3-12(2)

This hexachord, called by some the "magic" hexachord, is used in Schoenberg's *Ode to Napoleon Bonaparte*. It is one of two hexachords that can be segmented into a multiplication of the "augmented" trichord type 3-12-[0,4,8]: [0,4,8] × i(1), i(3), or i(5). These relations can also be expressed inversionally. The hexachord also contains more instances of the type 3-11-[0,3,7] than any other hexachord does. If we call $\{0,4,7\}$ (the C major triad) P_0, then 6-20 also contains its T_4 (the E major triad), T_8 (the A-flat major triad), I_3 (the A-flat minor triad), I_7 (the C minor triad), and I_{11} (the E minor triad). Multiplicatively, the hexachord can be partitioned into $\{0,3,7\}$ and its I_9. It can occur as a mode that alternates ip(1) and ip(3), just as 8-28 alternates ip(1) and ip(2).

6.16. Melody for 6-20-[0,1,4,5,8,9]. 3-11-[0,3,7] = $\{2,5,9\}$ + its I_3 = $\{1,10,6\}$ = $\{1,2,5,6,9,10\}$

16. 6-35

    [0,2,4,6,8,10]

    Sixth order all-combinatorial: *six* transpositions and *six* transposed inversions
        produce the complement

    Transpositionally and inversionally symmetrical

    Two different pitch class collections

    Interval vector $<0,6,0,6,0,3>$

    Trichord subset content: 3-6(6), 3-8(12), 3-12(2)

The "whole-tone" hexachord can be segmented into two instances of 3-6-[0,2,4] × i(6), the "whole-tone" trichord type, or two instances of 3-12-[0,4,8] × i(2) or i(6). It maximizes i(2), i(4), and i(6).

6.17. Multiplicative melody for 6-35-[0,2,4,6,8,10]. 3-6-[0,2,4] = $\{3,5,7\}$ × i(6) = $\{9,11,1\}$ = $\{1,3,5,7,9,11\}$

EXERCISE 6.1: Earlier exercises amplified

a) As with trichords and tetrachords, the "modal" singing exercise (4.22) is invaluable in gaining familiarity with larger sets.

b) Identify sets according to the family of interval content outlined in chapter 5. (Family 1 contains i(1), family 2 contains i(2) but not i(1), family 3 contains neither.)

c) Identify sets according to their membership in the two transpositions of the whole-tone set, as outlined in chapters 4 and 5. (Determine how many members of the set are in each of the two transpositions of the whole-tone set.)

d) Of all of these identification exercises for larger pitch class sets, perhaps most helpful is one involving superset family relationship: if you cannot identify a specific set, at least try to say if it is a diatonic subset, an octatonic subset, a whole-tone subset, a chromatic trichordal or tetrachordal superset, an "augmented triad" superset, or some combination of these. Gaining increased familiarity with the fifteen sets cited above makes them valuable as poles of orientation as well.

e) Different transpositions should be played of common larger sets such as the diatonic and octatonic collections. Students should then identify the nature of the transposition and the number of common pitch classes between transpositions. This simulates the thinking that goes on in twelve-tone operations.

EXERCISE 6.2: Partitioning

A trichord is played; sing a trichord that will complete a given hexachord. For example, an instance of [0,4,8]-3-12 is played; sing a version of this trichord type that will complete [0,1,4,5,8,9]-6-20, the "magic hexachord." This will have to be either T_1 or T_{11} of the first trichord.

EXERCISE 6.3: Exercises with musical examples

a) **Listen to exx. 54–56: what is the set class of each phrase element?**
b) **Listen to ex. 11: identify the pitch class set that occurs between reiterations of first pitch, including that pitch. What is the pitch class set of mm. 3–4? If we omit the highest and lowest pitches, what is the pitch class set represented?**
c) **Listen to ex. 8: the collection formed by the pitch classes of this melody is a subset of which common superset? It is a superset of which common subset(s)?**
d) **Listen to ex. 72: subdivide the eighteen attacks of this opening into 4 + 5 + 4 + 5. Classify each group with respect to subset and superset family relationships, and define each pc set class.**
e) **Listen to ex. 7: what is the total pc set formed by this melody? Play I_6 (C = 0). How many pitch classes are in common with the original?**
f) **Listen to ex. 102: subdivide the twelve attacks into 5 + 3 + 4. Identify the rip<( )> , CC, and set class of each group. Try to define any subset and superset relationships between these groups, in terms of either pitch class or contour class.**
g) **Listen to ex. 156: what pitch class set represents the union of the sets presented by the first measure of the alto flute part and the first two measures of the trumpet part?**
h) **Listen to all of ex. 156: what common larger collection contains the pitch classes of this passage?**

Although we have used normal order as presented in the names of set classes as a means of identifying harmonic entities, it is clear that this ordering is no more than a theoretically convenient contrivance. It has no musical significance if it is connected to neither registral order nor temporal order. There is however a large body of twentieth-century music for which a "tonic" pitch plays a central role. In such a context, giving such a central pitch the value 0 has strong musical significance.

DEFINITION 6.2: *Modal order*   For a group of pitches or pitch classes to be arranged in modal order signifies that the most strongly emphasized pitch, one that acts as a gravitational center, is given a value of 0, and that the values of the other pitches are derived from their distance in semitones from this central pitch.

The large body of folk-influenced music is one area where "tonic" pitch plays a central role, but the search for new modes is also one of the eternal pursuits of the twentieth-century composer. I have therefore used the device of M.O. <0, . . . >, a pitch class collection in which 0 is the pitch class that has the central role. A collection using the "white-key" (diatonic) collection and centered on C (the C major scale) would be represented by M.O. <0,2,4,5,7,9,11>. Centricity in a musical passage is created by metric emphasis, repetition, symmetrical approach, registral prominence (particularly low registral prominence), and other gravitational means. In twentieth-century music harmonic progression in the familiar sense is not necessarily the means available for the defining of a pitch center.

In Bartók's music, for example, a pitch center is almost always present. Moreover, Bartók was interested in creating chromatic or nearly chromatic densities through the device of *polymodality*.

DEFINITION 6.3: *Polymodality*   We call polymodality the superimposition of two different modes with the same tonal center.

In diatonic music, the use of the "melodic" minor with its "two versions" of the sixth and seventh scale degrees can also be seen as the same kind of phenomenon. In earlier music, however, the melodic minor is used not for the purpose of creating density, but for inflection toward a pitch goal. Pieces in the minor mode that use these two "versions" of the sixth and seventh scale degrees can nevertheless be conceived of as polymodal superimpositions of M.O. <0,2,3,5,7,8,10> and M.O. <0,2,3,5,7,9,11>.

EXERCISE 6.4: More exercises with musical examples

  a) Listen to ex. 28 (mm. 1–2). If we view the first pitch as a "tonic," what is the modal order that incorporates all the pitches? What is the normal order name of the pc set?
  b) Listen to ex. 41: what is the modal order for the entire collection of pitch classes in this passage?
  c) Listen to ex. 23 (mm. 1–3). The last pitch is the "tonic," and there are two "versions" of one scale degree. We can therefore conceive of the pitches as a superimposition of two M.O. forms. What are they?
  d) Each of the three two-bar segments of the sequential passage of mm. 7–12 of the same piece incorporates two versions of two modal degrees. If we combine all the pitches present, a six-note chromatic cluster results at the "bottom" of the mode. What are the two M.O. forms produced by the alternative versions of these modal degrees?
  e) Listen to ex. 10: there are two "versions" of one modal degree. Which M.O. is presented in mm. 5–8? In mm. 9–12?
  f) Listen to ex. 151. What is the M.O. of the right-hand mode? Of the left-hand mode?
  g) If we describe the pitch class content of the right hand as P_0, then which transformation can describe the left hand's pitch class content?
  h) If the shared "tonic" of the two modes is 0, which pc is absent from the passage?

Although many theorists treat the language of sets and the language of modes and centricity as if they were irreconcilable, this is not necessarily valid. The modal treatment of a pitch collection is often a centric treatment as described by its modal order, but it is always characterized by a *"flattened" treatment of the intervals: in modal motion and processes, the intervals between the scale steps of the mode are treated as if they were equivalent.* Emphasis is placed on the modal step as a unit regardless of the varying size of the unit within the mode. This is a strong undercurrent in the literature of diatonic tonality: Chopin's "Thirds Etude" begins with an alternation between B and D-sharp, and C-sharp and E; they are treated as "parallel" thirds even though one is ip(4) and the other is ip(3). (One could contrast the strongly functional or directional aspects of diatonic tonality, such as the leading-tone motion, with its modal aspects.) Modal treatment of pitch collections is similarly evidenced in the Russian Dance from Stravinsky's *Petrouchka,* where the piano writing treats the diatonic set modally by "equalizing" the set classes 3-10-[0,3,6] and 3-11-[0,3,7], by moving among the scale degrees of the mode without differentiating between half-steps and whole-steps.

By means of modal processes the equal-interval sets 3-12-[0,4,8], 4-28-[0,3,6,9], 6-35-[0,2,4,6,8,10], and the total chromatic set are made the model for other interval groupings, because modal steps act as though they span equal intervals. As an example of modal flattening we may treat the collection {0,1,3,5,8,9} modally, which would mean first to assign a "tonic" pitch class, and then to view the collection as scalar. To return to the image of a clock (see chapter 2), it would be imperative to construct a clock with six numbers on it. The pitch classes {0,1,3,5,8,9} would be mapped onto *degrees,* or "hours" on the clock: 0 (= 12 o'clock), 1, 2, 3, 4, 5. Under these modal conditions one could move (for example) in "parallel thirds," using the scale steps of the mode: the pitch class simultaneity {0,3} (= degrees 0,2) would move to {1,5} (= degrees 1,3), then to {3,8} (= degrees 2,4), then to {5,9} (= degrees 3,5), even though the intervals of the simultaneities vary from (3) to (4) to (5). Parallel motion in this context means keeping the *modal interval* M.I.(n) constant.

DEFINITION 6.4: *Modal interval*   Modal interval measures the number of *mode steps* between two degrees of a mode, regardless of the size of the pitch interval between the two steps. Like pitch interval or pitch class interval it has ordered and unordered forms. *Unordered modal interval* $(= M.I.(n))$ is the distance between two mode degrees regardless of order, calculated by counting the number of mode degrees between the two pitches. *Ordered modal interval* $(= M.I.+/-n)$ is the distance between two successive tones that act as mode degrees, calculated by counting the number of mode degrees between the first and second pitches of a modal melody. The symbol + designates an upward direction, and − a downward direction.

In a modal context the common expression "parallel thirds" really means keeping modal interval M.I.(2) constant. In the mode of C major, "C moving up to A" exemplifies M.I. $<+5>$, regardless of pitch interval. Proficiency in performing the following keyboard exercises will make one comfortable with a modal handling of pitch space.

EXERCISE 6.5: Keyboard exercise (for one)

a) Treat the following pc sets modally by playing two-voiced scales in "parallel thirds," that is, with the two voices at a distance of "modal interval two" (M.I.(2)). The scales should ascend two octaves or more and then descend. Do the same exercise with "parallel fourths" (M.I. (3)).

1. $\{0,+1,+4\}$: 3-3
2. $\{0,+4,+6,+9\}$: 4-27
3. $\{0,+2,+4,+7,+9\}$: 5-35
4. $\{0,+1,+3,+4,+6,+7,+9,+10\}$: 8-28
5. $\{0,+4,+10,+13,+21\}$: 5-16

b) Map the degree progression $<0-4-2-3-1>$ onto the pitch set $\{0,+1,+3,+6,+9\}$. Transfer the degree progression onto other pentads of your choice.

c) Make up more extended modal interval successions, and apply them to sets of 6 or 7 elements (for example, to all the sets mentioned earlier in this chapter). Try to identify the modal interval succession, the identity of the modal degrees (given a "0" pitch), and the pitch class set.

In its flattening of pitch and pitch class space, modal interval is similar to the contour interval that can be derived from the Contour Class (see chapter 3). Modal processes are closely related to contour processes.

DEFINITION 6.5: *Modal inversion* · Modal inversion applies to the signs of an ordered modal interval series. For example, with the collection $\{0,2,4,7,9\}$ modal inversion would turn the pc line $<2-4-7-4-9-7-4>$ (equivalent to the degree succession $<1-2-3-2-4-3-2>$, where 0 is seen as degree 0, 2 as degree 1, 4 as degree 2, and so on) into the pc line $<7-4-2-4-0-2-4>$ (equivalent to the degree succession $<3-2-1-2-0-1-2>$.

DEFINITION 6.6: *Modal sequencing* Modal sequencing preserves the ordered modal interval succession of a modal melody, but at different degree levels in the same mode.

DEFINITION 6.7: *Modal transposition* Modal transposition preserves the ordered modal interval succession of a modal melody, but uses a mode with a different pitch class set. The thematic development of Bartók's Music for

Strings, Percussion, and Celesta makes extensive use of modal transposition. The concept of modal space gives us another approach toward familiarity with the world of larger pitch class sets. One of the most realistic approaches to these larger sets is to sing the sets as modal degree successions, play modal sequences and parallelisms, and thus gain access to their pitch class interval content and set class identity.

The approach to melodic ideas that use modal processes is multidimensional:

EXERCISE 6.6: Exercises with modal melodies

In this exercise work with exx. 2, 6, 39 (mm. 1–3), 40, and 69.

a) Try to identify the relevant pitch class set type, and any prominent interval and subset properties that grow out of the interval content.

b) If there is a "tonic," try to identify a modal order in which the pitch classes can be arranged.

c) Try to assign degree numbers to the different pitch classes of the melodic passage, and define a modal degree progression that characterizes the passage. This approach does not depend on perceptions regarding set class.

d) In relating this passage to others, identify the processes of modal sequencing, modal transposition, and modal inversion.

The following exercise uses modal transposition to generate additional trichord melody possibilities:

EXERCISE 6.7: Singing modal transpositions (for one or more)

a) Sing a trichord melody from chapter 4, such as the one written for 3-3-[0,1,4].

b) Mentally assign the modal degree numbers 0, 1, and 2 to the pitch classes performing the functions of [0], [1], and [4].

c) Mentally assign those same degree numbers to pitch classes performing the functions of [0], [2], and [4] in any transposition of the trichordal set class 3-6-[0,2,4].

d) Sing the resulting melody, which represents a modal transposition of the trichord melody.

e) Any of the trichord melodies should be "transposable" in this manner to any other trichord type. This exercise will facilitate an understanding of modal thinking, as well as a more complete grasp of the trichord types.

f) More advanced students can perform the same exercise on the tetrachord melodies of chapter 5.

EXERCISE 6.8: Exercises dealing with the musical examples

a) Example 122: Listen to the left hand alone of mm. 1–3. Identify the pitch class set type that encompasses all of the pitches. If you view the lowest-sounding pitch as a "tonic," assign degree numbers to all the pitches. What is the modal interval succession?

b) In the same piece, listen to the left hand of mm. 7–9 juxtaposed with the left hand of mm. 1–3. What is the relation between their pitch class set types (unordered)? What is the relation of their modal interval succession?

c) Listen to ex. 150 (mm. 1–7). The bass line of these bars presents a scale segment of which mode?

d) Listen to four bars of ex. 155. Identify the polymodal element. (Which pitch of the oboe line in the fourth bar is dissonant with the mode of the first three bars?) What are the two other modal orders (with E-flat as the "tonic 0")?

Appendix I: Musical Examples

The following musical excerpts are adapted from the works of Debussy, Bartók, Stravinsky, and Schoenberg. They should be used constantly as a resource in sight-singing (including practice in pitch transposition and inversion) and dictation. Beyond that they should be used for recognizing and identifying both structures (set classes, rips, modes, contour classes) and processes (transposition and inversion).

The five groups of examples are organized as follows: groups 1–3 are made up of melodies for one voice; group 4 is made up of duets; group 5 is made up of examples with more than two voices. Within each group examples are ordered with respect to progressive difficulty.

Group 1

Stravinsky, *Petrouchka,* "Danse russe," mm. 1–8, flute

Debussy, Preludes for Piano, book 1, no. 6, "Footsteps in the Snow," mm. 2–5

Debussy, *La Mer,* mm. 12–17

Debussy, *Images*, "Hommage à Rameau," mm. 1–2

Stravinsky, *Rite of Spring*, from the third bar after rehearsal number 56 to the eighth bar after, alto flute solo

Debussy, Preludes for Piano, book 2, no. 5, "Bruyères," mm. 1–4, right hand

Debussy, *Prélude à l'après-midi d'un faune*, mm. 55–58, woodwind melody

Debussy, *Prélude à l'après-midi d'un faune*, mm. 37–38, oboe melody

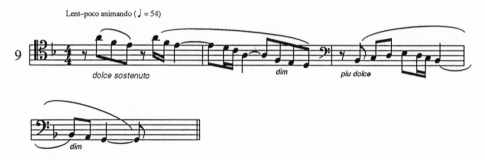

Debussy, Cello Sonata, first movement, mm. 8–11

Bartók, *Mikrokosmos,* vol. 5, no. 128, mm. 5–12, right hand

Debussy, *Prélude à l'après-midi d'un faune,* mm. 1–4

Prélude à l'après-midi d'un faune, m. 27

Debussy, Sonata for flute, viola, and harp, Interlude, mm. 1–4, flute; mm. 4–7, harp

Stravinsky, *L'Histoire du soldat,* "Little Concert," m. 1, cornet
Reprinted by permission of Editions Wilhelm Hansen.

Debussy, Cello Sonata, second movement, mm. 15–19, piano, right hand

Debussy, *Children's Corner,* "Little Shepherd," mm. 1–4, right hand

Debussy, Preludes for Piano, book 1, no. 3, "Le vent dans la plaine," mm. 3–6, left hand

Stravinsky, *L'Histoire du soldat,* "Little Concert," mm. 19–24, violin
Reprinted by permission of Editions Wilhelm Hansen.

Bartók, Concerto for Orchestra, second movement, beginning

20

Bartók, *Contrasts,* second movement, mm. 1–5, violin

21

Bartók, Divertimento for String Orchestra, second movement, mm. 2–5

Group 2

Schoenberg, *Ode to Napoleon Bonaparte,* op. 41, mm. 76–77, viola

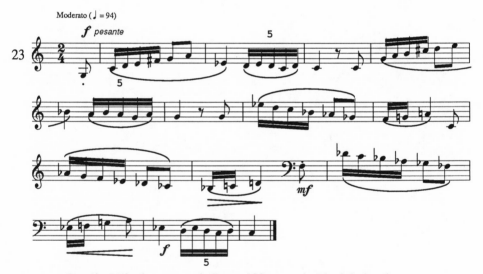

Bartók, *Mikrokosmos,* vol. 5, no. 130, mm. 1–14, right hand

Debussy, *La Mer,* third movement, mm. 60–63, two oboes

Bartók, Two Elegies, op. 8b, second elegy, mm. 5–7

Debussy, Sonata for flute, viola, and harp, Interlude, mm. 1–4, flute

Debussy, *La Mer,* first movement, mm. 122–26, cello solo

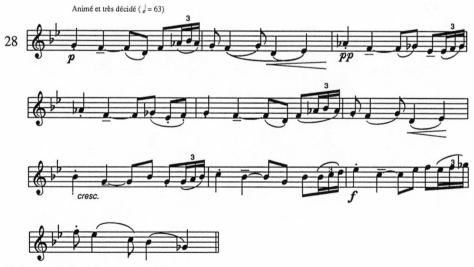

Debussy, String Quartet, first movement, mm. 26–35, first violin

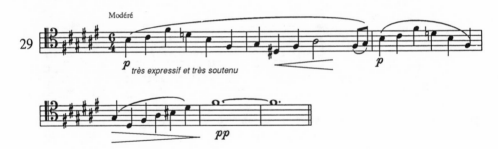

Debussy, *Nocturnes,* "Nuages," mm. 71–76, cello solo

Bartók, Concerto for Orchestra, fourth movement, mm. 1–9

Debussy, *Iberia,* mm. 194–202, flute

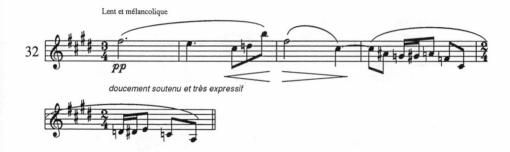

Debussy, Preludes for Piano, book 2, "Feuilles mortes," mm. 1–4

Bartók, *Contrasts,* third movement, mm. 134–37

Debussy, Cello Sonata, second movement, mm. 1–4

Bartók, String Quartet no. 1, mm. 1–5, first violin

Bartók, *The Wooden Prince*, p. 206, oboe

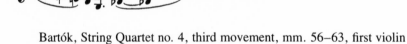

Bartók, String Quartet no. 4, third movement, mm. 56–63, first violin

Bartók, Solo Violin Sonata, third movement, mm. 1–6

Bartók, *Contrasts,* first movement, beginning, clarinet

Bartók, String Quartet no. 4, first movement, mm. 19–21

41

Bartók, Violin Concerto, opening of violin solo

42

Bartók, Violin Concerto, mm. 194–97

43

Bartók, Violin Concerto, mm. 73–76

44

Bartók, Violin Concerto, mm. 77–80

45

Schoenberg, Three Piano Pieces, op. 11, no. 1, mm. 1–11, right hand

Debussy, *Les fêtes galantes,* "Clair de Lune," mm. 5–8

Debussy, *Suite bergamasque,* "Clair de Lune," mm. 1–8

Bartók, Concerto for Two Pianos, Percussion, and Orchestra, second movement, mm. 5–8, piano

Stravinsky, *Firebird Suite,* mm. 1–2, cellos

Stravinsky, *Octet,* second movement, mm. 1–8

Stravinsky, *Firebird Suite,* "Infernal Dance," rehearsal number 100

Schoenberg, String Quartet no. 3, first movement, opening ostinato figure

Bartók, Piano Concerto no. 3, first movement, mm. 76–84, flute

Bartók, Music for Strings, Percussion, and Celesta, mm. 1–5

Bartók, Music for Strings, Percussion, and Celesta, first movement, mm. 69–73, third and fourth violins

Bartók, Music for Strings, Percussion, and Celesta, five-note melodic groups from fourth movement, mm. 195–204

57

Bartók, Music for Strings, Percussion, and Celesta, fourth movement, mm. 204–09, violin theme

58

Schoenberg, Three Songs, op. 48, no. 1, "Sommermüd," mm. 1–3, voice

59

Schoenberg, Three Songs, op. 48, no. 1, "Sommermüd," mm. 4–6, voice

60

Bartók, Viola Concerto, beginning

61

Schoenberg, Chamber Symphony, op. 9, mm. 16–19

Schoenberg, Chamber Symphony, op. 9, rehearsal number 80, mm. 1–4, violin

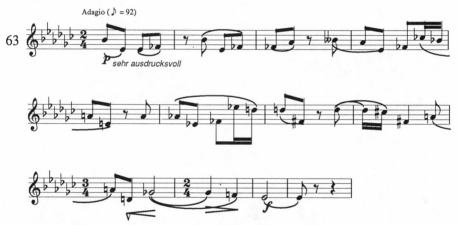

Schoenberg, Chamber Symphony, op. 38, Adagio, flute solo
Reprinted by permission of G. Schirmer, Inc.

Bartók, String Quartet no. 6, theme, mm. 1–13

Stravinsky, *Symphony of Psalms,* first movement, opening

Stravinsky, Elegy for Violin or Viola, mm. 1–4

Bartók, String Quartet no. 3, mm. 1–5, first violin

Stravinsky, *Symphony of Psalms,* second movement, mm. 1–4, oboe

Stravinsky, *Firebird,* rehearsal numbers 141 to 142, first violin

Schoenberg, String Quartet no. 4, third movement, beginning, mm. 1–5
Reprinted by permission of G. Schirmer, Inc.

Schoenberg, Three Songs, op. 48, no. 2, "Tot," mm. 4–8, voice

Schoenberg, Piano Concerto, mm. 1–7, right hand

Schoenberg, Variations for Orchestra, theme, mm. 1–5

Schoenberg, String Quartet no. 4, first movement, mm. 1–5, first violin
Reprinted by permission of G. Schirmer, Inc.

Schoenberg, Woodwind Quintet, op. 26, third movement, beginning, horn

Schoenberg, String Quartet no. 4, first movement, mm. 155–56, first violin   Reprinted by permission of G. Schirmer, Inc.

Stravinsky, *In Memoriam Dylan Thomas*, Song, mm. 3–6, tenor

Stravinsky, *In Memoriam Dylan Thomas*, Song, mm. 13–18, tenor

Schoenberg, String Quartet no. 4, second movement, mm. 292–94
Reprinted by permission of G. Schirmer, Inc.

80

Schoenberg, Chamber Symphony, op. 9, from one bar before rehearsal number 17 to three bars after, E-flat clarinet

81

Schoenberg, Variations for Orchestra, op. 31, variation 11, mm. 130–39

82

Schoenberg, *Ballade,* op. 12, no. 1, beginning

83

Debussy, *Les fêtes galantes II,* "Les ingénus," mm. 3, 4, 14, 16, 27–29, piano part; mm. 37–38, alto line of piano part

Group 3

Stravinsky, *Pribaoutki,* third movement, "Le colonel," mm. 1–6, clarinet

Reprinted by permission of Editions Wilhelm Hansen.

Stravinsky, Three Pieces for Clarinet, first movement, mm. 1–9

Schoenberg, String Quartet no. 2, op. 10, fourth movement, voice, mm. 74–78

87

Schoenberg, *Book of the Hanging Gardens,* op. 15, song 5, mm. 1–9, voice

88

Debussy, Etudes for Piano, book 1, no. 3, mm. 25–29, left hand

89

Schoenberg, Five Pieces for Orchestra, op. 16, no. 2, "Vergangenes," A clarinet

90

Schoenberg, *Accompaniment to a Cinematographic Scene,* op. 34, mm. 19–23

Schoenberg, *Drei Satiren,* op. 28, "Am Scheideweg," mm. 1–3

Schoenberg, Three Piano Pieces, op. 11, no. 2, mm. 16–19

Schoenberg, *Pierrot lunaire,* song 11, "Rote Messe," m. 1, piano ostinato

Schoenberg, Chamber Symphony, op. 38, mm. 11–19, first violin

Reprinted by permission of G. Schirmer, Inc.

95

Schoenberg, Song, op. 14, no. 1, "Ich darf nicht danken," mm. 3–7

96

Schoenberg, *Die glückliche Hand,* mm. 9–11, first female voice

97

Schoenberg, *Pierrot lunaire,* song 1, "Mondestrunken," mm. 15–18, violin

98

Schoenberg, Chamber Symphony, op. 9, last five bars

99

Schoenberg, String Quartet no. 2, fourth movement, mm. 51–55

100

Schoenberg, *Pierrot lunaire,* song 2, "Columbine," mm. 1–5, violin

101

Schoenberg, Wind Quintet, mm. 1–7, flute

102

Schoenberg, Five Piano Pieces, op. 23, no. 5, mm. 1–3

103

Stravinsky, Sonata for Piano, first movement, mm. 1–6

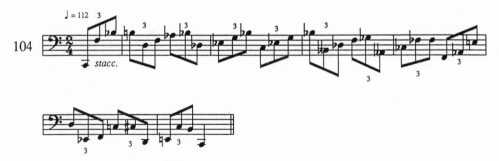

104

Stravinsky, Sonata for Piano, first movement, mm. 6–12

105

Stravinsky, Sonata for Piano, first movement, mm. 41–50

Stravinsky, *Abraham and Isaac,* mm. 12–18

Stravinsky, *A Sermon, a Narrative, and a Prayer,* Narrative, mm. 142–50, tenor

Bartók, Solo Violin Sonata, first movement, mm. 125–29

109

Schoenberg, *Pierrot lunaire,* "Mondestrunken," m. 1

110

Schoenberg, *Pierrot lunaire,* song 7, "Der kranke Mond," mm. 23–25, flute

111

Schoenberg, String Quartet no. 3, fourth movement, mm. 14–18, cello

112

Schoenberg, String Quartet no. 3, fourth movement, mm. 119–23

113

Stravinsky, *A Sermon, a Narrative, and a Prayer,* Narrative, mm. 113–16

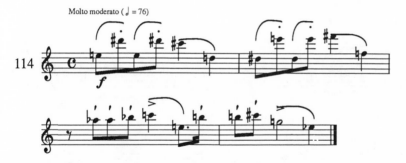

Schoenberg, String Quartet no. 3, fourth movement, mm. 1–4, first violin

Schoenberg, String Quartet no. 4, mm. 270–73, first violin

Reprinted by permission of G. Schirmer, Inc.

Schoenberg, Phantasy for Violin and Piano, mm. 1–4, violin

Schoenberg, *Serenade,* op. 24, Menuet, beginning, mm. 1–5

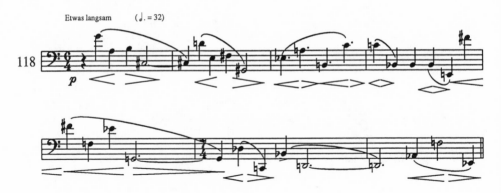

Schoenberg, Wind Quintet, third movement, mm. 1–7, bassoon

Schoenberg, Suite, op. 29, first movement, mm. 70–77, viola

Group 4: Duets

Bartók, *Mikrokosmos,* vol. 1, no. 36, mm. 1–9

Bartók, *Mikrokosmos,* vol. 4, no. 101, "Diminished Fifths," mm. 1–11

Bartók, *Mikrokosmos,* vol. 5, no. 123b, mm. 1–13

Stravinsky, *Threni,* Diphona II, mm. 114–19, violas and cellos

Stravinsky, *Threni,* Diphona II, mm. 114–17, first and second violins

Bartók, *Mikrokosmos,* vol. 5, no. 124, mm. 1–13, 30–36

126

Debussy, Nocturnes, "Nuages," mm. 1–4, two clarinets

127

Debussy, *Chansons de Bilitis,* "La chevelure," m. 1

128

Stravinsky, *Threni,* De Elegia Tertia, m. 174, tenor and bass

Stravinsky, *Threni,* Diphona I, mm. 66–67, two tenors

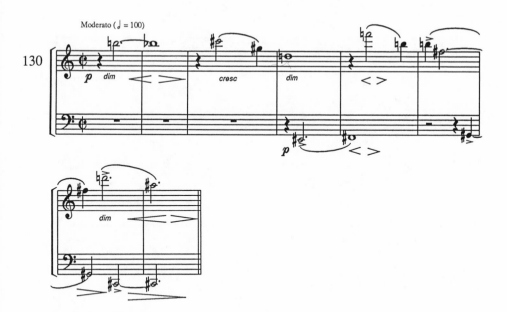

Schoenberg, String Quartet no. 3, first movement, mm. 5–12, first violin and cello

Stravinsky, *Symphonies of Wind Instruments,* rehearsal numbers 15 to 18, first flute and second clarinet

Schoenberg, String Quartet no. 2, fourth movement, opening

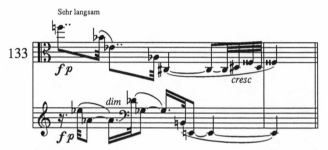

Schoenberg, String Quartet no. 2, op. 10, fourth movement, mm. 3–4, viola and cello

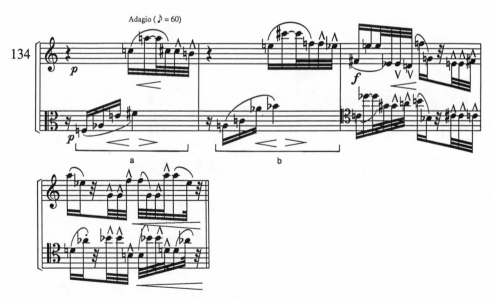

Schoenberg, String Quartet no. 3, second movement, mm. 92–93, first violin and viola; mm. 94–95, second violin and cello

Stravinsky, *Epitaphium*, m. 2, flute and clarinet

Stravinsky, *Epitaphium,* mm. 4–5, flute and clarinet

Schoenberg, Piano Piece, op. 33b, mm. 1–2

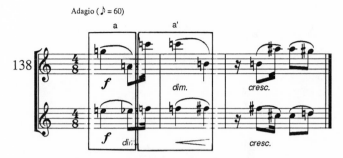

Schoenberg, String Quartet no. 3, second movement, mm. 1–3, first and second violins

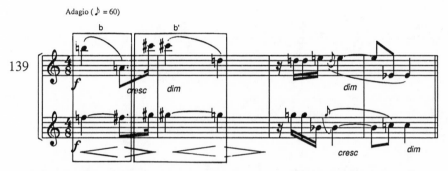

Schoenberg, String Quartet no. 3, second movement, mm. 6–9, first and second violins

Group 5: For More than Two Voices

Debussy, *Prélude à l'après-midi d'un faune,* mm. 4–5 (harmonies as verticalities)

Bartók, *Mikrokosmos,* vol. 5, no. 132, mm. 1–2, 22–24

Stravinsky, Three Pieces for String Quartet, first piece, mm. 1–10

Stravinsky, *Le roi des étoiles,* mm. 6–7

Stravinsky, *Symphonies of Wind Instruments,* first three bars after rehearsal number 21, two oboes and English horn

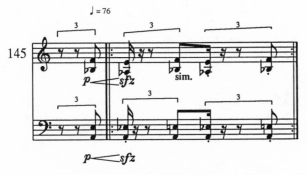

Stravinsky, Three Pieces for String Quartet, second piece, first two chords

Schoenberg, Three Piano Pieces, op. 11, no. 3, m. 15

Schoenberg, Suite for Piano, op. 25, Musette, mm. 14–15

148

Schoenberg, *Pierrot lunaire,* song 6, "Madonna," mm. 1–3, flute, bass, clarinet, and cello

149

Bartók, String Quartet no. 6, third movement, mm. 1–7

Bartók, *Mikrokosmos,* vol. 6, no. 149, mm. 1–6, 12–18

Bartók, *Mikrokosmos,* vol. 6, no. 148, mm. 3–8

Stravinsky, *Three Songs from Shakespeare,* song 2, "Full fadom five," piano transcription, m. 1

Stravinsky, *Threni,* m. 180, first tenor, first and second basses

Stravinsky, *Rite of Spring,* "Danse des adolescentes," first 4 bars after rehearsal number 14, English horn, bassoon, and cellos

Stravinsky, *Rite of Spring,* first 4 bars after rehearsal number 49

Stravinsky, *Rite of Spring,* first 9 bars after rehearsal number 131 (Kalmus edition), alto flute, trumpet, and bassoon

Stravinsky, *Rite of Spring,* first 2 bars after rehearsal number 100, three horns

Stravinsky, *Rite of Spring,* first 3 bars after rehearsal number 100, three oboes

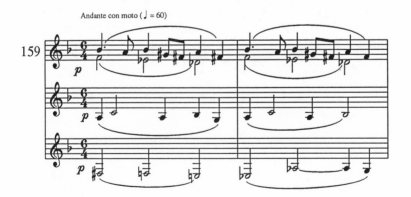

Stravinsky, *Rite of Spring,* first 2 bars after rehearsal number 99, four horns

160

Stravinsky, *Requiem Canticles*, m. 69

161

Stravinsky, *Requiem Canticles*, mm. 71–76

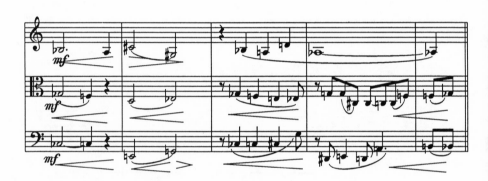

Schoenberg, String Trio, op. 45, episode 1, mm. 52–61

Schoenberg, String Trio, op. 45, mm. 267–72

164

Schoenberg, String Trio, mm. 292–93

165

Schoenberg, String Quartet no. 4, second movement, mm. 518–23

Reprinted by permission of G. Schirmer, Inc.

Stravinsky, Octet, rehearsal numbers 51 to 52, clarinet and two bassoons

167

Stravinsky, *In Memoriam Dylan Thomas,* mm. 1–6, four trombones

168

Stravinsky, *In Memoriam Dylan Thomas,* mm. 6–8, string quartet

169

Schoenberg, Three Piano Pieces, op. 11, no. 1, mm. 42–44

Schoenberg, String Quartet no. 4, first movement, mm. 1–16, three accompanying voices

Stravinsky, *Symphonies of Wind Instruments*, third part, three clarinets, two oboes, English horn, and three clarinets

Schoenberg, Violin Concerto, first movement, mm. 1–8, solo violin and cellos   Reprinted by permission of G. Schirmer, Inc.

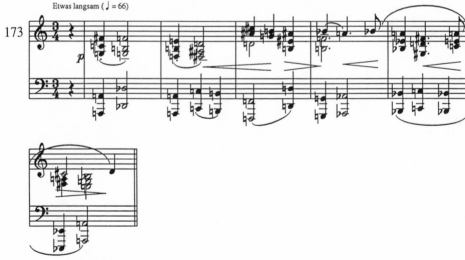

Schoenberg, *Book of the Hanging Gardens,* song 5, mm. 1–6, piano

Stravinsky, Three Pieces for String Quartet, third piece, mm. 3–16

Schoenberg, *Pierrot lunaire,* song 4, "Eine blasse Wäscherin," piano
reduction, m. 6

Schoenberg, *Pierrot lunaire,* song 4, "Eine blasse Wäscherin," piano reduction, m. 7

Schoenberg, *Pierrot lunaire,* song 4, "Eine blasse Wäscherin," piano reduction, m. 14

Schoenberg, *Pierrot lunaire,* song 4, "Eine blasse Wäscherin," piano reduction, mm. 15–16

Stravinsky, Septet, second movement, Passacaglia, mm. 9–17, clarinet, horn, and bassoon

Appendix II: Additional Exercises

This appendix contains four additional groups of exercises applied to several musical examples. The exercises are intended to develop skills in the aural perception of transformations and serve as applications in the recognition of structures and processes that have been introduced in the earlier chapters.

Group 1

In this section, when a phrase element is made of an inversionally symmetrical set class or contains one, that phrase element is enclosed in square brackets [ ] (see ill. app. 1a). After the entire melody is practiced vocally or

App. 1a. Inversionally symmetrical set classes: 3-6-[0,2,4]

instrumentally, the inversion that *preserves the pitch class content of the inversionally symmetrical set class* should be sung with pitch class numbers to underline the property of invariance, or played instrumentally. There are two distinct but equally relevant ways to do this: (1) Perform *the pitch class inversion that is also a pitch inversion*—the one in which *the contour as well as the pitch classes are inverted* (see ill. app.1b). This will highlight the

App.1b. *Pitch inversion* (including *contour inversion*)

process of inversion because of the "mirror relation" of the two melodies. (2) Perform *the pitch class inversion that preserves all the pitches of the inversionally symmetrical set class represented in the original melody* (see ill. app.1c). This will highlight the *pitch invariance relation of the two melodies,* but not necessarily the process of inversion.

App.1c. *Pitch class inversion* with *pitch invariance*

EXERCISE APP.1: Inversional symmetry and invariance

The four following melodies selected from the examples in appendix 1 contain bracketed fragments that exemplify inversionally symmetrical set classes. Invert the melodies vocally (with pitch class numbers) or instrumentally, so that the bracketed fragments hold the pitch class content invariant. This should be done in the two ways exemplified by ills. app.1b and app.1c.

Schoenberg, Three Lieder, op. 48, no. 2, "Tot," mm. 3–8

Bartók, String Quartet no. 3, first movement, mm. 1–5, first violin

Schoenberg, String Quartet no. 3, op. 30, second movement, mm. 1–3

Bartók, Music for Strings, Percussion, and Celesta, mm. 1–5

Group 2

In this section, when two fragments exemplify repetitions of the same set class they are enclosed in square brackets [   ] (see ill. app.2a). A kind of invariance relation occurs when one transposes the pitch classes that make for the first instance of such a set class so that the pitch classes of the second instance occur, and when one transposes the pitch classes that make for the

App.2a. Transposition

second instance of the set class so that the pitch classes of the first instance occur. After the entire melody is practiced vocally or instrumentally, it should be sung with pitch class numbers to underline the property of invariance, or played instrumentally. The student should sing the original and both transpositions of the melody often enough to hear this process. Again there are two ways

App.2b. *Pitch transposition* (including *contour invariance*): 3-8-[0,2,6]

to perform the transposition relation: perform *the pitch class transposition that is also a pitch transposition,* thus preserving contour (see ill. app.2b), and perform *the pitch transposition that preserves the pitches* of the passage with which the relation occurs (see ill. app.2c).

App.2c. *Pitch class transposition* with *pitch invariance*

EXERCISE APP.2: Transpositional invariance

The five following melodies selected from the examples in appendix 1 contain bracketed fragments that exemplify transpositionally related set classes. Transpose the melodies vocally (with pitch class numbers) or instrumentally, so that the first bracketed fragment of the transposition contains the same pitch class content as the second does in the original, and then so that the second bracketed fragment of the transposition contains the same pitch class content as the first does in the original. Each of the transpositions should be done in the two ways exemplified by ills. app.2b and app.2c.

Schoenberg, *Pierrot lunaire,* "Der kranke Mond," mm. 33–35, flute

Schoenberg, String Quartet no. 3, op. 30, fourth movement, mm. 119–23

Stravinsky, *A Sermon, a Narrative, and a Prayer,* Narrative, mm. 113–14

Bartók, Violin Concerto no. 2, mm. 79–82, solo violin

Stravinsky, Three Pieces for String Quartet, second piece, m. 1

Group 3

In this section, when two fragments exemplify repetitions of the same set class they are enclosed in square brackets [ ] (see ill. app.3a). These two fragments are related by the process of inversion, *though not necessarily*

App.3a. Inversion

ordered inversion. The student should sing the original and the inversion of the melody with pitch class numbers or play them instrumentally, to hear the *exchange of pitch class content* that takes place between the two melodic segments. Again there are two ways to perform the inversion: perform *the pitch class inversion of each of the two passages that is also a pitch inversion, thus creating exact contour inversion* (see ill. app.3b); and perform *the pitch class*

App.3b. *Pitch inversion* (including *contour inversion*)

inversion that preserves the pitches of the passage with which the relation occurs (see ill. app.3c).

App.3c. *Pitch class inversion* with *pitch invariance*

EXERCISE APP.3: Inversion and pitch class exchange

The six following melodies selected from the examples in appendix 1 contain bracketed fragments that exemplify inversionally related set classes. Invert the melodies vocally (with pitch class numbers) or instrumentally, so that there is an exchange of pitch class content between the two bracketed fragments. Each of the transpositions should be done in the two ways exemplified by ills. app.2b and app.2c.

Debussy, *Prélude à l'après-midi d'un faune*, m. 27, flutes

Schoenberg, String Quartet no. 4, op. 37, first movement, mm. 1–5, first violin
Reprinted by permission of G. Schirmer, Inc.

Schoenberg, String Quartet no. 4, op. 37, first movement, mm. 155–56, first violin
Reprinted by permission of G. Schirmer, Inc.

Schoenberg, String Quartet no. 4, op. 37, first movement, mm. 270–73, first violin
Reprinted by permission of G. Schirmer, Inc.

Schoenberg, String Quartet no. 3, op. 30, fourth movement, mm. 14–18, cello

Schoenberg, *Pierrot lunaire*, "Eine blasse Wäscherin," m. 14

Group 4

In this section, each melody either contains a bracketed fragment, or exemplifies in its entirety the occurrence of (1) the diatonic mode, (2) the pentatonic mode, (3) the whole-tone mode, (4) the octatonic mode, (5) the mode based on the "magic hexachord," or (6) the "chromatic" mode. These segments of the melody should be practiced and transformed into each of the other five modes through the process of mode-mapping described in chapter 6 and exemplified in ills. app.4a–f. This will familiarize students with the characteristics of the modes and the processes of modal transformation.

App.4a. Mode-mapping: *diatonic*

App.4b. Mode-mapping: *pentatonic*

App.4c. Mode-mapping: *whole-tone*

App.4d. Mode-mapping: *octatonic*

App.4e. Mode-mapping: *"magic"*

App.4f. Mode-mapping: *chromatic*

EXERCISE APP.4: Mode-mapping: writing and performing

The seven following melodies selected from the examples in appendix 1 contain bracketed fragments or represent in their entirety one of the six modes named above. After practicing the original melody, practice writing out mappings into each' of the remaining five modes and then perform them, either singing these transformations with pitch class numbers or playing them instrumentally.

Bartók, *Mikrokosmos,* vol. 5, no. 123b, mm. 2–4, right hand

Bartók, *Mikrokosmos,* vol. 1, no. 36, mm. 1–4, right hand

Bartók, *Mikrokosmos,* vol. 5, no. 128, mm. 5–12, right hand

Debussy, String Quartet, op. 10, first movement, mm. 1–2

Debussy, *Prélude à l'après-midi d'un faune,* mm. 37–38, oboe

Stravinsky, Octet, second movement, mm. 1–4, flute, clarinet

Stravinsky, *Firebird Suite,* "Infernal Dance," rehearsal number 100

Notes

CHAPTER 2: *Dyads*

1. Extensive theoretical treatment of dyads consistent with the sections that follow is found in John Rahn, *Basic Atonal Theory* (New York: Longman, 1980), 19–40.

2. According to the octave numbering system of the Acoustical Society of America, this pitch is called C4—the fourth-highest C on the piano keyboard. The choice of any pitch as 0 is subject to change as warranted by musical context, priorities in order, and the like.

3. The significance of dividing interval types into odd and even categories has to do with membership in the two whole-tone scales. Two pitches that form an even-numbered interval are in the same whole-tone scale; those that span an odd-numbered interval are in different whole-tone scales.

CHAPTER 3: *Processes*

1. Further exercises of this kind can be found in Rahn, *Basic Atonal Theory,* 46–47.

2. Rahn, *Basic Atonal Theory,* 90–91.

3. For fuller exploration of the implications of contour relationships see Michael L. Friedmann, "A Methodology for the Discussion of Contour: Its Application to Schoenberg's Music," *Journal of Music Theory* 29, no. 2 (1985): 223–48.

CHAPTER 4: *Trichords*

1. The interval vector has an interesting property: its numbers tell us how many common pitch classes there are between the different transpositions of a set class. If there are two instances of i(2) in a set class, the second number of the interval vector, then a transposition of the set by either 2 or 10 will have two pitch classes in common with the original form of the set. In the case of i(6), the number of pitch classes that the original set and its tritone transposition have in common is *double the sixth entry* in the interval vector. For example, 3-10-[0,3,6] has an interval vector of <0,0,2,0,0,1>. A transposition by 3 or 9 of three pitch classes forming this set class will show *two* pitch classes in common with the first form. Note however that a transposition by 6 will also show two pitch classes in common with the first form: because of the symmetrical nature of i(6) we must double the sixth digit of the interval vector to predict the number of common tones in transpositions by six.

2. The notion of hearing representatives of set classes in terms of their membership in the distinct transpositions of "equal-interval" sets such as the whole-tone scale was inspired by Andrew Mead, "Pedagogically Speaking: A Practical Method for Dealing with Unordered Pitch-Class Collections," *In Theory Only* 7, nos. 5–6 (March 1984).

3. The fullest treatment of segmentation in post-tonal music can be found in Christopher Hasty's article "Segmentation and Process in Post-Tonal Music," *Music Theory Spectrum* 3 (1981): 54–73.

CHAPTER 5: *Tetrachords*

1. For a discussion of the interpretive powers of multiplication (called by him transpositional combination) and inversion see Richard Cohn, "Inversional Symmetry and Transpositional Combination in Bartók," *Music Theory Spectrum* 5, no. 10 (1988).

Glossary

COMBINATORIALITY (definition 6.1). The equal partitioning of the twelve pitch classes—among four forms of a single trichordal set class type that are equivalent transpositionally, inversionally, or both; among three such forms of a single tetrachord set class type; or between two such forms of a single hexachordal set class type. In this book we have been concerned only with hexachordal combinatoriality. A hexachord is therefore said to be combinatorial when there exists one or more transpositions *or* one or more inversions of it that produce its complement. Thus the original collection of six pitch classes and one transposition or inversion of it combine to result in all twelve pitch classes. A collection of pitch classes of which the transposition(s) *and* inversion(s) are capable of producing the complement of a given collection of six pitch classes is said to exhibit *all-combinatoriality*. The "order" of an all-combinatorial set class is defined as the number of transpositions or inversions that produce its complement. Thus *first-order all-combinatoriality* results when *one* transition and *one* inversion of a collection of six pitch classes produce the complement of the collection, *second-order all-combinatoriality* results when *two* transpositions and *two* inversions produce the complement, and so on.

CONTOUR ADJACENCY SERIES (CAS; definition 3.7). The CAS is an ordered series of + and − signs corresponding to each up and down of a melodic line. The *inversion* of a CAS is the inversion of its + and − signs. Thus CAS <+,+,−,−,+,+,−> inverted is CAS <−,−,+,+,−,−,+>.

CONTOUR CLASS (CC; definition 3.9). An ordered series of integers that indicate the registral position of a pitch in a musical unit: 0 indicates the lowest pitch of a musical unit, 1 the second-lowest pitch, and n − 1 the highest (where n is the number of different pitches in the musical unit). Inversion of a CC, its mirror image, is accomplished by mapping each contour element to its opposite: the highest CC element becomes 0, the lowest n − 1, the second-highest 1, and so on. The index number for an element of a CC and its inversion is always n − 1.

DEGREE OF SYMMETRY (definition 4.13). The number of operations on a melodic or harmonic structure or on a set class that leaves its pitch classes invariant.

DIATONIC SCALE OR COLLECTION (definition 4.3). The set type of seven pitch classes that can be expressed as the major scale, the natural minor scale, the "white-key collection," [0,1,3,5,6,8,10], and 7-35. It is the complement of the pentatonic collection.

DYAD (definition 2.1). A harmony constituted of two tones.

FORTE NUMBER. *See* SET CLASS.

INTERVAL. The interval, or pitch class interval, is the distance between two pitch classes. An ordered, or directed, pitch class interval (i<n>) is the distance between two successive pitch classes, calculated by subtracting the pitch class number of the first pitch class from the pitch class number of the second pitch class. If the second pitch class number is lower than the first, the number 12 is added to it before the subtraction is performed. If one visualizes the numbers of the twelve pitch classes as the numbers on the face of a clock, the ordered pitch class interval is found by measuring the *clockwise* distance between the two pitch classes. The size of i<n> ranges from 1 to 11. An unordered pitch class interval (i(n); definition 2.8) is the distance between two pitch classes regardless of order, calculated by subtracting the lower pitch class number from the higher pitch class number. If the result is higher than 6 the result is subtracted from 12, because the size of i(n) ranges from 1 to 6. To continue the analogy with the clock face, the unordered pitch class interval is found by measuring the shortest distance between the two pitch classes, clockwise or counterclockwise. *See also* MODAL INTERVAL; PITCH INTERVAL.

INTERVAL VECTOR (definition 4.9). A listing of the frequency with which the six unordered interval types occur in a pitch class set or set type. The first digit of the interval vector indicates the frequency of i(1) in the set, the second digit indicates the frequency of i(2), and so on. Any trichords with the same interval vector are of the same set class type. Set classes with more than three elements may have the same interval vector, but are of a different set class type (*see* Z-RELATED SETS).

INVARIANCE (definition 3.6). The common element(s) between musical units related by a process such as transposition or inversion.

INVERSION. The polarization of one or more dyads of *pitches or pitch classes* about an axis. *Pitch inversion* (definition 3.3) is the mirroring of a pitch or pitches about an axial pitch. To invert a pitch about a given axis, one measures the distance of the pitch from the axis and finds the corresponding pitch the same distance from the axis in the opposite direction, producing a symmetrical structure. One defines $I_{+/-n}^P$ as pitch inversion where the sum of each pitch and its inversion will be $+/-n$. *Pitch class inversion* (definition 3.4) mirrors *pitch classes* about a pair of axes. The procedure follows that of pitch inversion, except that pitch classes are used instead of pitches. Pitch class inversion of pitch class n about axis 0 is defined as $12 - n$. I_n is a pitch class inversion according to which the sum of each pitch class and its inversion will be n.

INVERSIONAL SYMMETRY (definition 4.12). A pitch class set can be characterized as inversionally symmetrical in two ways. A pitch class set is inversionally symmetrical if there is a spatial arrangement for it of which the rip<( )> forms a PALINDROME. A pitch class set is also inversionally symmetrical if its elements can be inverted so that there is complete pitch class invariance between the original representation of the set and a particular inversion.

MAGIC HEXACHORD. The hexachord type [0,1,4,5,8,9]-6-20. (For further information on this hexachord see chapter 6.)

MAPPING. The transformation of each of the elements of a set by an operation such as transposition or inversion. Mapping is also used in normalization processes for pitch class sets.

MAXIMIZATION (of an interval). The occurrence of a given i(n) type with the greatest possible frequency in a set of a given number of elements. For example, in a set of three elements there can be no more than two instances of i(1). We can therefore say that 3-1-[0,1,2] *maximizes* i(1).

MODAL INTERVAL (definition 6.4). A measure of the number of *mode steps* between two degrees of a mode, regardless of the size of the pitch interval between the two steps. As with pitch interval mod 12, there are ordered and unordered forms.

MODAL ORDER (definition 6.3). A method of describing the elements of a *modal* set class with the *central* pitch given the number 0, and the other elements accordingly numbered in ascending order.

MODAL SEQUENCING (definition 6.6). The shifting of a series of *modal degrees* to a different position in the same mode, thus preserving the *modal interval* series of a melodic idea.

MODAL TRANSPOSITION (definition 6.7). The shifting of a series of *modal intervals* from a mode representing one pitch class set to a mode representing another pitch class set.

MULTIPLICATION (definition 5.2). I(p) multiplied by i(q) can be said to occur when two instances of i(p) are separated by i(q). Symmetrical tetrachords can be generated by the multiplication of two dyads.

NORMALIZATION (*see* definition 4.7). The process of testing for equivalence by placing symbols for pitch class sets in *normal order* (also called best normal order).

NORMAL ORDER. *See* definition 4.7 and SET CLASS.

OCTATONIC SCALE OR COLLECTION (definition 4.6). The set of eight pitch classes that can be expressed as a scale with alternating whole-steps and half-steps, as the combination of any two different diminished seventh chords, as [0,1,3,4,6,7,9,10] or 8-28. There are three distinct transpositions of the octatonic collection.

PALINDROME (*see* definition 3.1). A symmetrical entity of which the retrograde is the same as the original; also, an idea and its retrograde.

PENTATONIC SCALE OR COLLECTION (definition 4.4). The set of five pitch classes that can be expressed as the black-key collection, [0,2,4,7,9] or 5-35. It is the complement of the diatonic collection.

PITCH (definition 2.2). The specific fundamental as defined on the staff, as played by instrumentalists and sung by singers. If one assigns numbers to pitches, "middle C" below the treble clef (and above the bass clef) can be called 0. Pitches above middle C are given positive (+) numerical values corresponding to their distance in half-steps from middle C; pitches below middle C are given negative (−) numerical values corresponding to their distance in half-steps from middle C.

PITCH CLASS (definition 2.7). A numerical name for a category of pitches separated by 0 semitones, 12 semitones, or any multiple of 12 semitones. There are 12 possible pitch classes, numbered from 0 to 11. The number 0 can be considered equivalent to C (or B-sharp or D-double flat) in a fixed naming system, or it can be considered another central pitch class as determined by a musical context.

PITCH INTERVAL. The distance between two pitches, measured in semitones. There are four forms. An *ordered pitch interval* (ip<n>; definition 2.4) is the distance between two successive pitches, calculated by counting the number of semitones between the two pitches and indicating upward or downward direction by a plus (+) or minus (−); ip<n> can be any positive or negative integer. An *unordered pitch interval* (ip(n); definition 2.3) is the distance between two pitches regardless of order, calculated by counting the number of semitones between the two pitches; ip(n) can be any integer. An *ordered pitch interval mod 12* (ip mod 12<n>; definition 2.6) is the distance between two successive pitches, calculated by counting the number of semitones between two pitches, indicating upward or downward direction by a plus (+) or minus (−), and reducing the resulting integer by 12 until it is a number between 1 and 11. An *unordered pitch interval mod 12* (ip mod 12(n); definition 2.5) is the distance between two pitches regardless of order, calculated by counting the number of semitones between two pitches and then reducing the resulting integer by 12 until it is a number between 1 and 11.

POLYMODALITY (definition 6.3). The simultaneous combination of *two or more different modes with the same pitch class as their center.*

REGISTRAL PITCH INTERVAL SERIES (rip series, rip$<(n_1,n_2,\text{etc.})>$; definition 4.11). The pitch intervals of a musical unit in order from bottom to top.

RETROGRADE (definition 3.1). The reversal of the temporal order of a succession of pitches or pitch classes.

SEGMENTATION (definition 4.14). An analytic process that divides musical continuity into intelligibly related parts.

SET CLASS (definitions 2.9, 4.1). The fundamental harmonic structure of post-tonal music. The members of a set class have the same subset content and can be related by the operations of either transposition or inversion. Each set class is defined by two names: its *normal order name* (known elsewhere in the theoretical literature as the *best normal order* name or *Tn/TnI* form), which is discovered through the process of normalization; and its "*Forte-number*" *name*, a two-digit name used commonly in the analytical literature. The best normal order name (definition 4.8) for a set class is a symbolic series derived from the most compact ordering of the pitch classes in the set class. In this symbolic series the first element is called [0] and the other elements are numbered according to their distance from the first element. The "Forte number" (definition 4.10) for a set class is composed of two digits separated by a hyphen. The first integer specifies the number of different pitch classes in the set class, the second the position of the set on Forte's list of set classes.

TRANSPOSITION (definition 3.2). The addition of a constant interval to a group of pitches or pitch classes. *Pitch transposition* $T_{+/-n}^{p}$ of a melodic idea preserves contour. If n is understood as the number of semitones, then + n indicates upward transposition and − n downward transposition. *Pitch class transposition* T_n does not necessarily preserve contour. If n is understood as the number of clockwise steps on the face of a clock, then T_n is pitch class transposition by a number n ranging from 1 to 11.

WHOLE-TONE SCALE OR COLLECTION (definition 4.5). The set of six pitch classes that can be expressed as a scale made up of whole-steps, as [0,2,4,6,8,10] or 6-35. There are two distinct transpositions of the whole-tone collection.

Z-RELATED SETS (definition 5.1). Two set classes are said to be a Z-related pair if they have the same interval content as shown in their interval vector, but not the same normal order name. The members of a Z-related pair have different trichord subset contents and characteristics of superset membership, and are related neither by transposition nor by inversion. The only tetrachordal Z-related pair consists of [0,1,4,6]-4-Z15 and [0,1,3,7]-4-Z29, the all-interval tetrachords.

Music Acknowledgments

I wish to express my gratitude to the following for permission to reprint musical examples:

To Boosey and Hawkes, Inc., for the following works of Stravinsky:

Le Sacre du printemps © 1921 by Edition Russe de Musique; copyright assigned to Boosey & Hawkes, Inc.

Three Pieces for String Quartet © 1922 by Edition Russe de Musique; copyright assigned to Boosey & Hawkes, Inc.

Sonata for Piano © Edition Russe de Musique; copyright assigned to Boosey & Hawkes, Inc.

A Sermon, a Narrative, and a Prayer © 1961 by Boosey & Co., Ltd.

Octet for Winds © by Edition Russe de Musique; copyright renewed. Copyright and renewal assigned to Boosey & Hawkes, Inc. Revised version © 1952 by Boosey & Hawkes, Inc.; copyright renewed.

Elegy © 1944 by Boosey & Hawkes, Inc.; copyright renewed.

Abraham and Isaac © 1965 by Boosey & Hawkes Music Publishers, Ltd.

Symphony of Psalms © 1931 by Edition Russe de Musique; copyright renewed. Copyright and renewal assigned to Boosey & Hawkes, Inc.

Revised edition copyright by Boosey & Hawkes, Inc.; copyright renewed.

Threni © 1958 by Boosey & Co., Ltd.; copyright renewed.

In Memoriam Dylan Thomas © 1954 by Boosey & Hawkes, Inc.; copyright renewed.

Symphonies of Wind Instruments © 1926 by Edition Russe de Musique; copyright assigned to Boosey & Hawkes, Inc. Revised version © 1952 by Boosey & Hawkes, Inc.; copyright renewed.

Septet © 1953 by Boosey & Hawkes, Inc.; copyright renewed.

Three Songs from Shakespeare © 1954 by Boosey & Hawkes, Inc.; copyright renewed.

Epitaphium © 1959 by Hawkes and Son (London), Ltd.; copyright renewed.

Petrouchka © by Edition Russe de Musique; copyright assigned to Boosey & Hawkes, Inc. Copyright renewed.

Requiem Canticles © 1967 by Boosey & Hawkes Music Publishers, Ltd.

To G. Schirmer, Inc., for the following works of Stravinsky:
L'histoire du soldat, reprinted by permission of Editions Wilhelm Hansen.
Pribaoutki, reprinted by permission of Editions Wilhelm Hansen.

To Belmont Music Publishers for the following works of Schoenberg:
String Quartet no. 2, op. 10
String Quartet no. 3, op. 30
Piano Piece, op. 33b
Pierrot lunaire, op. 21
Piano Concerto, op. 42
Three Piano Pieces, op. 11
Suite for Piano, op. 25
Chamber Symphony, op. 9
Variations for Orchestra, op. 31
Ballade, op. 12, no. 1
Wind Quintet, op. 26
Die glückliche Hand, op. 18
Drei Satiren, op. 28
Book of the Hanging Gardens, op. 15
String Trio, op. 45
Ich darf nicht danken, op. 14, no. 1
Ode to Napoleon Bonaparte, op. 41
Suite, op. 29

To C. F. Peters for the following works of Schoenberg:
  Phantasy for Violin and Piano © 1952 by Henmar Press, Inc. (C. F. Peters Corporation).
  Five Orchestra Pieces © 1952 by Henmar Press, Inc. (C. F. Peters Corporation).
  Accompaniment to a Cinematographic Scene © 1930 by Heinrichshofen's Verlag, Wilhelmshaven. Reprinted by permission of C. F. Peters Corp., sole selling agents.

To G. Schirmer, Inc., for the following works of Schoenberg:
  String Quartet no. 4, op. 37
  Violin Concerto, op. 36
  Chamber Symphony no. 2, op. 38

To Boelke-Bomart, Inc., and Mobart Music Publications for the following works of Schoenberg:
  Three Songs, op. 48 © 1952 by Bomart Music Publications, Inc.; copyright assigned 1955 to Boelke-Bomart, Inc. Revised edition © 1979 by Boelke-Bomart, Inc.

To Hal Leonard Publishing Corporation for the following work of Stravinsky:
  Firebird

To Boosey and Hawkes for the following works of Bartók:
  Music for Strings, Percussion, and Celesta © 1937 by Universal Editions; copyright renewed. Copyright and renewal assigned to Boosey & Hawkes, Inc., for the U.S.A.
  Violin Concerto no. 1 © 1946 by Hawkes & Son (London), Ltd.; copyright renewed.
  Mikrokosmos © 1940 by Hawkes & Son (London), Ltd.; copyright renewed.
  String Quartet no. 6 © 1941 by Hawkes & Son (London), Ltd.; copyright renewed.
  String Quartet no. 3 © 1929 by Universal Editions; copyright renewed. Copyright and renewal assigned to Boosey & Hawkes, Inc., for the U.S.A.
  String Quartet no. 1. Reprinted by permission of Boosey & Hawkes, Inc., sole agents for Kultura (Hungarian Trading Company) in the U.S.A.
  Concerto for Two Pianos © 1970 by Hawkes & Son (London), Ltd.
  Contrasts © 1942 by Hawkes & Son (London), Ltd.; copyright renewed. Reprinted by permission of Boosey & Hawkes, Inc.

Index

Adjacency, registral and temporal, 3–6
All-combinatoriality, 110 (def.), 111–13
All-interval tetrachords, 74, 90, 98
Analysis by ear, xxiii. *See also* Segmentation
Arpeggios
  tetrachordal, 99
  trichordal, 67–68
Axis (of pitch inversion, pitch class inversion), 27–30

Bartók, Béla, xxiii, xxv, 61, 79, 87, 91, 106, 116
  Concerto for Orchestra, 126, 130
  Concerto for Two Pianos, Percussion, and Orchestra, 135
  Contrasts, 127, 131, 133
  Divertimento for String Orchestra, 127
  Mikrokosmos
    vol. *1*, no. *36*, 82, 155, 192
    vol. *4*, no. *101*, 156
    vol. *5*, no. *123b*, 156, 192,
    vol. *5*, no. *124*, 157
    vol. *5*, no. *128*, 124, 192
    vol. *5*, no. *130*, 128
    vol. *5*, no. *132*, 164
    vol. *6*, no. *148*, 168
    vol. *6*, no. *149*, 168
  Music for Strings, Percussion, and Celesta, 36, 60, 137–38, 186

Piano Concerto no. *3*, 136
Solo Violin Sonata, 133, 151
String Quartet no. *1*, 132
String Quartet no. *3*, 140, 186
String Quartet no. *4*, 132, 133
String Quartet no. *6*, 139, 167
Two Elegies, op. *8b*, 129
Viola Concerto, 138
Violin Concerto, 134, 188
Wooden Prince, 132
Berio, Luciano, 45

Calisthenics, xxi, 3–7
Cohn, Richard, 195*n*
Consonance, 8, 38, 79
Contour, xx, xxii, xxiv–xxv, 33–37, 195*n*
  contour adjacency series, 33 (def.), 34, 36–37
  contour class, 34 (def.), 35–37
  contour improvisation, 36–37
  contour interval series, 35
  of trichords, 69–70

Debussy, Claude, xxiii, xxv, 105–06
  Cello Sonata, 123–25, 131
  Chansons de Bilitis, 158
  Children's Corner, "Little Shepherd," 126
  Etudes for Piano, 146
  Iberia, 130